Java EE 7 First Look

Discover the new features of Java EE 7 and learn to put them together to build a large-scale application

NDJOBO Armel Fabrice

BIRMINGHAM - MUMBAI

Java EE 7 First Look

First published: November 2013

Production Reference: 1121113

Published by Packt Publishing Ltd.
Livery Place
35 Livery Street
Birmingham B3 2PB, UK.

ISBN 978-1-84969-923-5

www.packtpub.com

Cover Image by Abhishek Pandey (abhishek.pandey1210@gmail.com)

Credits

Author
NDJOBO Armel Fabrice

Reviewers
Markus Eisele
E.P. Rama krishnan

Acquisition Editors
Sam Birch
Joanne Fitzpatrick

Commissioning Editor
Mohammed Fahad

Technical Editors
Ritika Singh
Nikhita K. Gaikwad

Project Coordinator
Ankita Goenka

Proofreader
Christopher Smith

Indexer
Monica Ajmera Mehta

Graphics
Yuvraj Mannari

Production Coordinator
Shantanu Zagade

Cover Work
Shantanu Zagade

About the Author

NDJOBO Armel Fabrice is a Design Computer Engineer and graduate from the National Advanced school of Engineering Cameroon, and Oracle Certified Expert, Java EE 6 Java Persistence API Developer. In the past, he has worked with Java EE to develop several systems among which are a helpline system and a commercial management application. He currently works on several systems based on EJB, Spring and ICEFaces solutions. In addition, he has made a technical review of the books *Pro Spring Integration* published by Apress and *Beginning EJB 3, Java EE* published by Apress. He is also a copywriter in `developpez.com` (his home page is: `http://armel-ndjobo.developpez.com/`).

First of all, I want to thank the Lord Jesus who makes everything possible for me. I would like to thank Dr. Georges Edouard Kouamou for making me love Software Engineering. I would like to thank Fomba Ken Collins for his critiques that have helped me improve the quality of the book. I would also like to thank Serge Tsala, Armel Mvogo, and my fiancée Ines Tossam who encouraged me during the writing of this book. And finally, I would like to express my gratitude to Licel Kenmue Youbi for all his efforts.

Credits

Author
NDJOBO Armel Fabrice

Reviewers
Markus Eisele
E.P. Rama krishnan

Acquisition Editors
Sam Birch
Joanne Fitzpatrick

Commissioning Editor
Mohammed Fahad

Technical Editors
Ritika Singh
Nikhita K. Gaikwad

Project Coordinator
Ankita Goenka

Proofreader
Christopher Smith

Indexer
Monica Ajmera Mehta

Graphics
Yuvraj Mannari

Production Coordinator
Shantanu Zagade

Cover Work
Shantanu Zagade

About the Author

NDJOBO Armel Fabrice is a Design Computer Engineer and graduate from the National Advanced school of Engineering Cameroon, and Oracle Certified Expert, Java EE 6 Java Persistence API Developer. In the past, he has worked with Java EE to develop several systems among which are a helpline system and a commercial management application. He currently works on several systems based on EJB, Spring and ICEFaces solutions. In addition, he has made a technical review of the books *Pro Spring Integration* published by Apress and *Beginning EJB 3, Java EE* published by Apress. He is also a copywriter in developpez.com (his home page is: http://armel-ndjobo.developpez.com/).

First of all, I want to thank the Lord Jesus who makes everything possible for me. I would like to thank Dr. Georges Edouard Kouamou for making me love Software Engineering. I would like to thank Fomba Ken Collins for his critiques that have helped me improve the quality of the book. I would also like to thank Serge Tsala, Armel Mvogo, and my fiancée Ines Tossam who encouraged me during the writing of this book. And finally, I would like to express my gratitude to Licel Kenmue Youbi for all his efforts.

About the Reviewers

Markus Eisele is a Principal Technology Consultant working for msg systems AG in Germany. He is a Software Architect, a Developer, and a Consultant. He also writes for IT magazines. He joined msg in 2002 and has been a member of the Center of Competence IT-Architecture for nine years. After that he moved on to the IT-Strategy and Architecture group. He works daily with customers and projects dealing with Enterprise-level Java and infrastructures. This includes the Java platform and several Web-related technologies on a variety of platforms using products from different vendors. His main areas of expertise are Java EE Servers. He speaks at different conferences about his favorite topics. He is also part of the Java EE 7 expert group.

Follow him on `twitter.com/myfear` or read his ramblings with Enterprise level software development at `http://blog.eisele.net`.

E.P. Rama krishnan is an enthusiastic freelance developer and a technical writer. He has steady industry exposure of 5 years. His areas of expertise include JSF (JavaServer Faces), Java Persistence API, CDI, RESTful Services, Swings, Tomcat Clustering, and Load-balancing. His other areas of interest are Linux, Android, and Systems security. Besides development his major interest lies in writing technical blogs which simplify the latest technologies for early adopters. You are welcome to visit his blog at `http://www.ramkitech.com` and feel free to give your feedback. He can be reached at `ramkicse@gmail.com`.

www.PacktPub.com

Support files, eBooks, discount offers and more

You might want to visit www.PacktPub.com for support files and downloads related to your book.

Did you know that Packt offers eBook versions of every book published, with PDF and ePub files available? You can upgrade to the eBook version at www.PacktPub.com and as a print book customer, you are entitled to a discount on the eBook copy. Get in touch with us at service@packtpub.com for more details.

At www.PacktPub.com, you can also read a collection of free technical articles, sign up for a range of free newsletters and receive exclusive discounts and offers on Packt books and eBooks.

http://PacktLib.PacktPub.com

Do you need instant solutions to your IT questions? PacktLib is Packt's online digital book library. Here, you can access, read and search across Packt's entire library of books.

Why Subscribe?

- Fully searchable across every book published by Packt
- Copy and paste, print and bookmark content
- On demand and accessible via web browser

Free Access for Packt account holders

If you have an account with Packt at www.PacktPub.com, you can use this to access PacktLib today and view nine entirely free books. Simply use your login credentials for immediate access.

Table of Contents

Preface   **1**

Chapter 1: What's New in Java EE 7   **5**

A brief history of Java EE   **5**
The main goals of Java EE 7   **6**
Productivity   7
HTML5 support   7
Novelties of Java EE 7   **8**
Summary   **10**

Chapter 2: New Specifications   **11**

Concurrency Utilities for Java EE 1.0   **11**
Why concurrency?   11
Benefits of concurrency   12
Risks of concurrency   12
Concurrency and Java EE   12
Java EE Concurrency API   12
Batch Applications for Java Platform 1.0   **17**
What is batch processing?   17
Why a dedicated API for batch processing?   18
Understanding the Batch API   18
JobRepository   19
Job   19
Step   19
Chunk   20
Batchlet   21
The batch.xml configuration file   22
JobOperator   22

Java API for JSON Processing 1.0   **23**
  What is JSON?   23
    Object   23
    Array   23
    Why JSON?   24
    Java API for JSON processing   25
Java API for WebSocket 1.0   **27**
  What is WebSocket?   28
  Why WebSocket?   28
  The WebSocket API   28
    Server endpoint   29
    Client endpoint   31
  Summary   **32**
Chapter 3: The Presentation Layer   **33**
  Servlet 3.1   **33**
  What is a Servlet?   33
    A login page with a Servlet   34
    Latest improvements of Servlet 3.1 in action   36
    Non blocking I/O API   36
    Protocol upgrade processing   39
  Expression Language 3.0   **41**
  What is Expression Language?   42
  The latest improvements of EL 3.0 in action   42
    API for standalone environments   43
    Lambda expressions   43
    Collection object support   44
  JavaServer Faces 2.2   **47**
  What is JavaServer Faces?   47
  An identification page with JSF   48
  The latest improvements of JSF 2.2 in action   50
    HTML5-friendly markup   50
    Resource Library Contracts   52
    Faces Flow   54
    Stateless views   57
  Summary   **57**
Chapter 4: The Java Persistence API   **59**
  Java Persistence API 2.1   **59**
  JPA (Java Persistence API)   59
  JPA in action   60
  The latest improvements of JPA 2.1 in action   62
    Persistence context synchronization   62
    Entity   63
    New annotations   64
    Entity graphs   65

JPQL	67
The Criteria API	69
DDL generation	70
Java Transaction API 1.2	**72**
The Java Transaction API	72
JTA in action	73
Innovations introduced by JTA 1.2	74
Summary	**75**
Chapter 5: The Business Layer	**77**
Enterprise JavaBeans 3.2	**77**
Pruning some features	78
The latest improvements in EJB 3.2	78
Session bean enhancement	79
EJB Lite improvements	81
Changes made to the TimerService API	82
Harmonizing with JMS's novelties	84
Other improvements	85
Putting it all together	**87**
Presenting the project	87
Use Case Diagram (UCD)	88
Class diagram	89
Component diagram	91
Summary	**92**
Chapter 6: Communicating with External Systems	**93**
JavaMail	**93**
Sending e-mails in Java	94
Sending an e-mail via the SMTP protocol	94
The latest improvements in action	96
The added annotations	96
The added methods	98
The changing of some access modifiers	98
Java EE Connector Architecture (JCA)	**99**
What is JCA?	99
JCA in action	100
Latest improvements	101
Java Message Service (JMS)	**101**
When to use JMS	101
The latest improvements in action	102
New features	102
Java API for RESTful Web Services	**105**
When to use Web Services	106
JAX-RS in action	106

The latest improvements in action	107
The Client API	107
Asynchronous processing	107
Filters and entity interceptors	110
Summary	**114**
Chapter 7: Annotations and CDI	**115**
Common annotations for the Java platform	**115**
The goal of this specification	115
Building your own annotation	116
Latest improvements in action	120
The new annotation	120
Contexts and Dependency Injection	**120**
What is CDI ?	121
Example 1 – instantiation of a POJO	121
Example 2 – accessing an EJB from a JSF page	122
Example 3 – setting a bean with a specific scope for simple operations	124
Example 4 – use of objects usually created by a factory	124
Latest improvements in action	125
Avoiding CDI processing on a bean	126
Accessing the non contexual instance of a bean	126
Accessing the current CDI container	127
Destroying CDI bean instances explicitly	127
Summary	**127**
Chapter 8: Validators and Interceptors	**129**
Bean Validation	**129**
Validating your data	129
Building a custom constraint	135
Creating a constraint annotation	135
Implementing a validator	136
Latest improvements in action	138
Openness	138
Support for dependency injection and CDI integration	138
Support for method and constructor validation	139
Support for group conversion	140
Support message interpolation using expression language	142
Interceptors	**143**
Intercepting some processes	143
Defining interceptors in the target class	143
Defining interceptors in an interceptor class	145
Latest improvements in action	146
Intercept constructor invocation	146
Associating an interceptor with a class using interceptor binding	147
Defining the execution order of interceptors	148
Summary	**149**

Chapter 9: Security	**151**
JASPIC 1.1	**151**
Secure access to forms	151
Implementing an authentication module	152
The latest improvements in action	**161**
Integrating the authenticate, login, and logout methods called	162
Standardizing access to the application context identifier	162
Support for forward and include mechanisms	163
Summary	**163**
Index	**165**

Preface

When we considered writing this book, the main objective was to present the new features of Java EE 7 platform. But while writing, we came to realize that it would be interesting to make a clear and concise presentation of the relevant specifications and how to implement them. This led us to imagine a project that will help present almost all the specifications affected by Java EE 7 and how to put them together in order to build a large-scale application.

In short, this book does not aim to show how to implement the different aspects of each Java EE 7 specification or list the best practices. Rather, it positions itself similar to the yellow pages for a city that has been built recently. In other words, this book will help you discover the innovations introduced by Java EE 7 and give you ideas to build solid applications.

What this book covers

Chapter 1, *What's New in Java EE 7*, gives an overview of the improvements made in the Java EE 7 platform.

Chapter 2, *New Specifications*, explains concepts concerning the new specifications that have been added in Java EE 7 and shows how they can be used.

Chapter 3, *The Presentation Layer*, demonstrates the implementation of the improvements brought by the Java EE 7 platform for the presentation layer specifications.

Chapter 4, *The Java Persistence API*, shows how your Java application can store and retrieve data from the database in a safe way and explains the innovations that have been made in the relevant specifications.

Chapter 5, *The Business Layer*, begins by giving a presentation of the improvement in the business layer and then demonstrates how various Java EE 7 specifications can be put together for the realization of an application.

Chapter 6, Communicating with External Systems, demonstrates how a Java EE 7 application can interact with heterogeneous systems.

Chapter 7, Annotations and CDI, explains how annotations and CDI can be used to improve the quality of applications.

Chapter 8, Validators and Interceptors, shows how the validation and interception of data can be implemented in a Java EE environment to ensure the quality of the data handled by an application.

Chapter 9, Security, demonstrates the implementation of security and setting up a personal module for security in Servlet and EJB containers.

What you need for this book

To implement the various examples present in this book, you will need the following software:

* NetBeans IDE 7.3.1 or higher
* JDK 7
* GlassFish Application Server 4, at least b89
* MySQL 5.5 or higher DBMS

Who this book is for

Given the main objectives, this book targets three groups of people who possess knowledge about Java. They are:

* Beginners in using the Java EE platform who would like to have an idea about the main specifications of Java EE 7
* Developers who have experimented with previous versions of Java EE and want to know what Java EE 7 has brought as novelties
* Budding architects who want to learn how to put together various Java EE 7 specifications for building robust and secure enterprise applications

Conventions

In this book, you will find a number of styles of text that distinguish between different kinds of information. Here are some examples of these styles, and an explanation of their meaning.

Code words in text, database table names, folder names, filenames, file extensions, pathnames, dummy URLs, user input, and Twitter handles are shown as follows: "We can include other contexts through the use of the `include` directive."

A block of code is set as follows:

```
@NameBinding
@Target({ ElementType.TYPE, ElementType.METHOD })
@Retention(value = RetentionPolicy.RUNTIME)
public @interface ZipResult {})
```

New terms and **important words** are shown in bold. Words that you see on the screen, in menus or dialog boxes for example, appear in the text like this: "Expand the **server-config** menu."

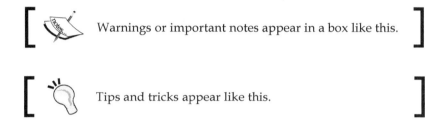

Warnings or important notes appear in a box like this.

Tips and tricks appear like this.

Reader feedback

Feedback from our readers is always welcome. Let us know what you think about this book—what you liked or may have disliked. Reader feedback is important for us to develop titles that you really get the most out of.

To send us general feedback, simply send an e-mail to feedback@packtpub.com, and mention the book title via the subject of your message.

If there is a topic that you have expertise in and you are interested in either writing or contributing to a book, see our author guide on www.packtpub.com/authors.

Customer support

Now that you are the proud owner of a Packt book, we have a number of things to help you to get the most from your purchase.

Downloading the example code

You can download the example code files for all Packt books you have purchased from your account at http://www.packtpub.com. If you purchased this book elsewhere, you can visit http://www.packtpub.com/support and register to have the files e-mailed directly to you.

Errata

Although we have taken every care to ensure the accuracy of our content, mistakes do happen. If you find a mistake in one of our books—maybe a mistake in the text or the code—we would be grateful if you would report this to us. By doing so, you can save other readers from frustration and help us improve subsequent versions of this book. If you find any errata, please report them by visiting http://www.packtpub.com/submit-errata, selecting your book, clicking on the **errata submission form** link, and entering the details of your errata. Once your errata are verified, your submission will be accepted and the errata will be uploaded on our website, or added to any list of existing errata, under the Errata section of that title. Any existing errata can be viewed by selecting your title from http://www.packtpub.com/support.

Piracy

Piracy of copyright material on the Internet is an ongoing problem across all media. At Packt, we take the protection of our copyright and licenses very seriously. If you come across any illegal copies of our works, in any form, on the Internet, please provide us with the location address or website name immediately so that we can pursue a remedy.

Please contact us at copyright@packtpub.com with a link to the suspected pirated material.

We appreciate your help in protecting our authors, and our ability to bring you valuable content.

Questions

You can contact us at questions@packtpub.com if you are having a problem with any aspect of the book, and we will do our best to address it.

What's New in Java EE 7 1

Because of their use, distributed applications require some non functional services such as remote access, security, transaction management, concurrency, and robustness, among others. Unless you have APIs that offer these types of services, you need to implement them all from scratch and therefore, increase the number of bugs, reduce software quality, and increase production costs and time. The Java EE platform was set up to save the developer from these concerns. It is made up of a set of APIs that facilitate the development and deployment of distributed, robust, scalable, and interoperable applications.

Since its first release in 1999, the Java EE platform has evolved over time by offering a newer, richer, and simpler version than the previous one. In order for you to have an overview of the improvements in Java EE 7, this chapter addresses the following topics:

- A brief history of Java EE
- The main goals of Java EE 7
- Novelties of Java EE 7

A brief history of Java EE

Formerly called J2EE, the first version of Java EE platform was officially released in December 1999 with 10 specifications. Among these specifications, there were Servlets and JavaServer Pages (JSP) for data presentation, **Enterprise JavaBeans (EJB)** for the management of persistent data, remote access to business services through RMI-IIOP (Remote Method Invocation over Internet Inter-ORB Protocol), and the JMS (Java Message Service) specification, which was used to send messages.

Despite efforts and many contributions, early versions of Java EE were too complex and difficult to implement. This led to much criticism and caused the rise of competing frameworks such as Spring Framework.

Having drawn lessons from its previous failures, the platform has considerably evolved over time until the production of Java EE 5, which permitted the platform to regain its lost esteem. From this version, Java EE continues to provide easier, richer, and more powerful versions of the platform.

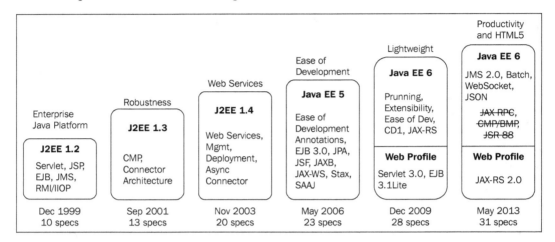

The preceding diagram gives an overview of the important changes made to Java EE platform since the release of the first version in December 1999. This diagram highlights the release dates, updates, and major improvements in each version. It also allows us to have an idea about the central theme behind each version.

The main goals of Java EE 7

Since May 2006, the Java EE platform has known remarkable evolution in terms of implementation. First, with Java EE 5, it greatly simplified the development of applications by allowing the transformation of a simple Java class (POJO class) into a business object through annotations or XML descriptions. Still in the line of simplification, Java EE 6 helps enrich annotations and introduces new concepts such as pruning, RESTful Web Services, CDI, EJB Lite, and configuration by exception and web profiles. This allows the platform to provide many easy-to-deploy and consume services. After the success of Java EE 6, the JCP (Java Community Process) envisaged turning the platform into a service by providing an infrastructure for cloud support. But, due to lack of significant progress in the concerned specifications, it revised its objectives. It is from the perspective of preparing the migration of the Java EE platform to the cloud that Java EE 7 focuses on productivity and HTML5 support. Having missed the big goal (that is, the migration to the cloud), it will reach its new goals through completion of Java EE 6 features and addition of some new specifications.

Productivity

Productivity in Java EE 7 has been improved upon in many ways. By simplifying some APIs such as JMS and JAX-RS, Java EE 7 platform significantly reduces boilerplate code. As you will notice in the chapters that follow, sending a JMS message can fit on one line and no longer requires the creation of several objects as was the case with JMS 1.1, where it was first necessary to create a `Connection`, `Session`, `MessageProducer`, and `TextMessage`.

Java EE 7 has integrated new APIs to better address the needs of enterprise applications relative to the processing of large amounts of data. We have, for example, the **concurrency utilities**, which allow the creation of managed threads within a container and give developers the ability to break down large processes into smaller units that can be computed concurrently. Similarly, there is a Java API for batch processing to manage bulk and long-running jobs.

Finally, Java EE 7 is enriched in annotations and has set a focus on configuration by exception. Whether it is for data source or batch processing, compatible Java EE 7 containers provide a number of default objects. It is even possible to produce complex applications with minor configuration.

In short, the new platform frees the developer from performing a number of tasks and the creation of several types of objects that are required for setting up an application.

HTML5 support

Some people might wonder why the support of HTML5 is so important. The answer is simple: HTML5 is the latest release of the HTML standard. More so, it offers new features that ease the building of more powerful and suitable web applications. For example, via the `<audio>` and `<video>` elements of HTML5, you can play, pause, and resume audio and video media content without the use of a third-party plugin such as Flash. Through the canvas element and WebGL library (a subset of OpenGL), you can easily integrate 2D and 3D graphics in your website. With regards to communication between the client and server, the perfect integration of WebSocket protocol in HTML5 allows us to build a web application with full-duplex P2P communication and get over some limitations of HTTP for real-time communication. Using this protocol, you will have no difficulty in realizing chat applications or other web applications that require real-time communication between the client and server, such as trading and e-commerce platforms. In terms of data exchange, the native support of JSON format in HTML5 simplifies processing of information and reduces the size of documents. Many other areas have been improved, but for now we will only mention these ones.

Given all these innovations, the support for HTML5 features was added in JSF (JavaServer Faces), a new API was added to Java EE 7 platform to build WebSocket-driven applications and another API to process JSON data format.

Novelties of Java EE 7

The Java EE 7 was developed as a Java Specification Request (JSR 342). It has a total of 31 specifications including 4 new specifications, 10 major releases, and 9 MRs (Maintenance Releases). All these specifications are taken into account by the GlassFish Server 4.0 (accessible via the address `https://glassfish.java.net/download.html`), which is the reference implementation of Java EE 7.

The new specifications introduced in Java EE are as follows:

- Concurrency Utilities for Java EE 1.0 (`http://jcp.org/en/jsr/detail?id=236`), for asynchronous processing and multi-threaded tasks in Java EE application components.
- Batch Applications for the Java Platform 1.0 (`http://jcp.org/en/jsr/detail?id=352`), to perform long-running tasks and bulk operations.
- Java API for JSON Processing 1.0 (`http://jcp.org/en/jsr/detail?id=353`), which provides support for JSON processing. It offers Java EE components the ability to parse, generate, transform, and query JSON format.
- Java API for WebSocket 1.0 (`http://jcp.org/en/jsr/detail?id=356`), to build WebSocket applications.

APIs inherited from the Java EE 6 platform that have undergone major changes are the following:

- Java Platform, Enterprise Edition 7 (Java EE 7) Specification (`http://jcp.org/en/jsr/detail?id=342`), when compared to Java EE 6, further simplifies development, adds support for HTML5, and prepares the platform to migrate to the cloud
- Java Servlet 3.1 Specification (`http://jcp.org/en/jsr/detail?id=340`) introduces some features such as non blocking I/O API and protocol upgrade processing
- Expression Language 3.0 (`http://jcp.org/en/jsr/detail?id=341`) was separated from JSP specification request, and it came with many changes including an API for standalone environments, lambda expressions, and collections objects support

- JavaServer Faces 2.2 (http://jcp.org/en/jsr/detail?id=344) integrates the support for the HTML5 standard and brings features such as resource library contracts, Faces Flow, and stateless views

- Java Persistence 2.1 (http://jcp.org/en/jsr/detail?id=338) brings us the opportunity to execute Stored Procedures, create named queries at runtime, construct bulk update/delete via the Criteria API, override or change the fetch setting at runtime, and make explicit joins as in SQL

- Enterprise JavaBeans 3.2 (http://jcp.org/en/jsr/detail?id=345) introduces the ability to manually disable the passivation of stateful session beans and has also relaxed rules to define the default local or remote business interface

- Java Message Service 2.0 (http://jcp.org/en/jsr/detail?id=343) simplifies the API

- JAX-RS 2.0: The Java API for RESTful Web Services (http://jcp.org/en/jsr/detail?id=339) simplifies the implementation of RESTful Web Services and introduces new features including Client API, asynchronous processing, filters, and interceptors

- Contexts and Dependency Injection for Java EE 1.1 (http://jcp.org/en/jsr/detail?id=346) introduces many changes, some of which are access to the current CDI container, access to the non contexual instances of a bean, and the ability to explicitly destroy bean instances

- Bean Validation 1.1 (http://jcp.org/en/jsr/detail?id=349) introduces support for method and constructor validation, group conversion, and message interpolation using expression language

Only the following APIs are affected by maintenance releases:

- Web Services for Java EE 1.4 (http://jcp.org/en/jsr/detail?id=109)

- Java Authorization Service Provider Contract for Containers 1.5 (JACC 1.5) (http://jcp.org/en/jsr/detail?id=115)

- Java Authentication Service Provider Interface for Containers 1.1 (JASPIC 1.1) (http://jcp.org/en/jsr/detail?id=196) standardizes the use of some aspects of the specification

- JavaServer Pages 2.3 (http://jcp.org/en/jsr/detail?id=245)

- Common Annotations for the Java Platform 1.2 (http://jcp.org/en/jsr/detail?id=250) adds a new annotation for managing priorities

- Interceptors 1.2 (http://jcp.org/en/jsr/detail?id=318) adds standard annotation for managing the execution order of interceptors

- Java EE Connector Architecture 1.7 (`http://jcp.org/en/jsr/detail?id=322`) adds two annotations for defining and configuring the resource adapter's resources

- Java Transaction API 1.2 (`http://jcp.org/en/jsr/detail?id=907`) provides the possibility to demarcate transactions declaratively and define beans whose lifecycle is identical to the current transaction

- JavaMail 1.5 (`http://jcp.org/en/jsr/detail?id=919`) slightly simplifies the development of sending an e-mail by adding annotations and methods

Summary

After briefly introducing the evolution of Java EE and analyzing the objectives of the latest platform, we listed all the specifications that were improved upon or added in Java EE 7. In the next chapter, we will focus on new specifications to highlight their usefulness and show how they can be implemented.

2
New Specifications

This chapter will only talk about new specifications that have been added in Java EE 7. In concrete terms, we will present and show how to use the following APIs:

- Concurrency Utilities for Java EE 1.0
- Batch Applications for Java Platform 1.0
- Java API for JSON Processing 1.0
- Java API for WebSocket 1.0

Concurrency Utilities for Java EE 1.0

Concurrency Utilities for Java EE 1.0 was developed under JSR 236. This section gives you only an overview of the API. The complete document specification (for more information) can be downloaded from `http://jcp.org/aboutJava/communityprocess/final/jsr236/index.html`.

Why concurrency?

In computer science, **concurrency** is the ability of an application or a system to execute many tasks in parallel. Before the advent of multitasking system, computers could only run one process at a time. At that time, the programs were not only difficult to design, but they were also executed sequentially from beginning to end and when the machine was running a program that had access to a peripheral device, the running program was first interrupted to allow the reading of the peripheral.

Benefits of concurrency

The development of multitasking operating systems enabled the simultaneous execution of many processes (instances of running programs) within a machine and many threads (also called lightweight processes; they are subsets of a process that can be run concurrently with each other) within a process. Due to this progress, it has become possible to run multiple applications at the same time, for example, listening to music and downloading a document while writing a text document.

In enterprise applications, concurrency can increase the interactivity of your program by running heavy processing asynchronously in a thread. It can also be used to improve the response time of an application by dividing a big task into smaller units that will be executed simultaneously by many threads.

Risks of concurrency

Although each thread has its proper stack of execution, it is very common to have multiple threads that share the same resources or depend on each other. In such cases, the absence of good synchronization makes threading behavior unpredictable and can degrade system performance. For example, the lack of coordination of interrelated threads can result in deadlocks and indefinitely interrupt processing.

Concurrency and Java EE

As we have seen previously, the misuse of threads can have catastrophic consequences on an application. In the case of a container, it could not only compromise its integrity, but also poorly exploit the resources provided to other components. This is one of the reasons why developers were not allowed to create threads in a container.

To enable implementation of concurrency within Java EE components, the Java EE 7 platform has integrated Concurrency Utilities. Using this API, a Java EE server can become aware of the resources that are used by threads and provide them with good execution context. Furthermore, it allows the server to manage the pool and lifecycle of threads.

Java EE Concurrency API

Concurrency Utilities for Java EE 1.0 was developed with the followings goals in mind:

- To provide a simple and flexible concurrency API to the Java EE platform without compromising the container

- To facilitate migration from Java SE to Java EE by providing consistency between the concurrency programming models
- To allow the implementation of common and advanced concurrency patterns

Concurrency Utilities was built over the Concurrency Utilities API developed under JSR-166 for Java SE (which facilitates the migration from Java SE to Java EE). It offers four main programming interfaces whose instances must be made available to application components as container-managed objects. The offered interfaces are: `ContextService`, `ManagedExecutorService`, `ManagedScheduledExecutorService`, and `ManagedThreadFactory`. All these interfaces are contained in the `javax.enterprise.concurrent` package.

These four interfaces can be explained as follows:

- **Managed executor service**: The `ManagedExecutorService` interface extends the `java.util.concurrent.ExecutorService` interface. It allows us to submit an asynchronous task that will be run on a separate thread created and managed by the container. By default, any Java EE 7-compliant server must provide a `ManagedScheduledExecutorService` that can be accessed by application components under the **JNDI** name `java:comp/DefaultManagedScheduledExecutorService`. But, if you want to create your own, you must first declare the `ManagedExecutorService` resource environment reference in the `web.xml` file for a web application or `ejb-jar.xml` for an EJB module. The specification recommends that all `ManagedExecutorService` resource environment references be organized in the `java:comp/env/concurrent` subcontext.

    ° The following configuration is an example declaration of a `ManagedExecutorService` resource environment reference:

```
<resource-env-ref>
  <resource-env-ref-name>
    concurrent/ReportGenerator
  </resource-env-ref-name>
  <resource-env-ref-type>
    javax.enterprise.concurrent.ManagedExecutorService
  </resource-env-ref-type>
</resource-env-ref>
```

- ○ After declaring the JNDI reference, you can then inject it by using
  the @Resource annotation as shown in the following code:

  ```
  @Resource(name="concurrent/ReportGenerator")
  ManagedExecutorService reportGenerator;
  ```

- ○ The task to submit to the container must either implement the java.
  lang.Runnable or java.util.concurrent.Callable interface.
  The differences between these interfaces are presented in the
  following table:

Runnable	Callable
Since JDK 1.0.	Since JDK 5.0.
It has run() method to define task.	It has the call() method to define task.
It is not generic and the run() method does not return any value.	It is generic and the call() method of a Callable<V> instance returns a value of type V.
The run() method cannot throw checked exception.	The call() method can throw checked exception.

- ○ The following code demonstrates how to define a task that will run
  reports asynchronously:

  ```java
  public class ReportGeneratorTask implements Callable<String>{

    @Override
    public String call() throws Exception {
      //generate report
      return "The report was generated successfully";
    }
  }
  ```

° The following code shows us how to submit a task. We can see that the `submit()` method of the `ManagedExecutorService` instance returns an object of type `Future` that will get back the result of the running task when it becomes available:

```
Future<String> monitor = reportGenerator
.submit(new ReportGeneratorTask());
String result = monitor.get();
```

- **Managed scheduled executor service:** The `ManagedScheduledExecutorService` interface extends the `ManagedExecutorService` and `java.util.concurrent.ScheduledExecutorService` interfaces in order to execute a task at a specific time.

° Instances of this interface are defined in the same way as that of the `ManagedExecutorService` interface. The following code demonstrates how to execute a task ten seconds after its submission:

```
Future<String> monitor = reportGenerator
  .schedule(new ReportGeneratorTask(), 10,
    TimeUnit.SECONDS);
```

- **Managed thread factory:** The `ManagedThreadFactory` interface provides method to create managed thread instances in a container. The task must implement the `java.lang.Runnable` interface. The following code demonstrates how to create and run a container-managed thread.

```
Thread myThread = threadFactory.newThread
  (new ReportManagedThread());
myThread.start();
```

- **Context service:** This interface allows the creation of contextual objects without using `ManagedExecutorService` or `ManagedScheduledExecutorService` interfaces, as we did in the previous cases, with the aim of allowing the extension of the capabilities of a Java EE platform for concurrency. Concretely, with this interface, you can create a workflow system or use customized Java SE platform `ExecutorService` implementations within a container. For example, if you desire to use the pool management mechanism provided by the class `java.util.concurrent.ThreadPoolExecutor` of Java SE to manage your threads in the context of a Java EE component, you will just need to combine `ManagedThreadFactory`, `ExecutorService`, and `ContextService` objects. The result is as shown in the following code:

```
public class ReportCustomizedThread implements Runnable {

  public void run() {
```

```
      //Report processing ...
  }
}

@Resource(name=»concurrent/ReportManagedThreadGenerator»)
ManagedThreadFactory threadFactory;

@Resource(name=»concurrent/ReportContextServiceGenerator»)
ContextService contextService;

ReportCustomizedThread reportThread = new
ReportCustomizedThread();
Runnable proxy =
  contextService.createContextualProxy(reportThread,
  Runnable.class);
ExecutorService executorService =
  Executors.newFixedThreadPool(20, threadFactory);
Future result = executorService.submit(proxy);
//...
```

This is probably a simple example of the use you can make of this feature. For more advanced examples, please consult the specification document in the *Context service* section.

The following diagram provides an overview of relationships between Concurrency Utilities and other Java EE platform elements:

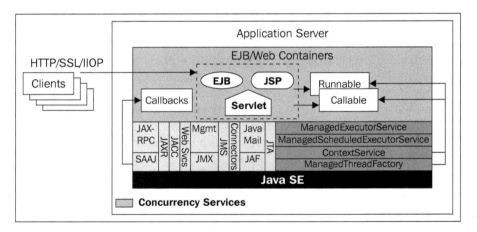

Besides, it is possible to refine the configurations of different resources for better performance (for details, see the specification document), and the Concurrency Utilities for Java EE 1.0 provide many other interfaces like ManagedTaskListener that can be used to monitor the state of a task's Future object.

Batch Applications for Java Platform 1.0

The Batch Applications API for the Java Platform 1.0 was developed under JSR 352. This section just gives you an overview of the API. The complete document specification (for more information) can be downloaded from http://jcp.org/aboutJava/communityprocess/final/jsr352/index.html.

What is batch processing?

According to the Cambridge Advanced Learner's Dictionary, a batch is a group of things or people dealt with at the same time or considered similar in type. And a process is a series of actions that you take in order to achieve a result. Based on these two definitions, we can say that **batch processing** is a series of repetitive actions on a large amount of data in order to achieve a result. Given the large amounts of data that it has to deal with, batch processing is often used for end of day, month, period, and year processing.

The following is a short list of domains where you can use batch processing:

- Data import/export from/to XML or CSV files
- Accounting processing such as consolidations
- ETL (**extract-transform-load**) in a data warehouse
- Digital files processing (downloading, processing, or saving)
- Notification of a service's subscribers (such as forum, group, and so on)

Why a dedicated API for batch processing?

After having an idea about batch processing, some people might ask themselves: Why not just set a `foreach` loop that launches many threads? First of all, you have to know that batch processing is not only concerned with the execution speed. Indeed, the processing of large amounts of data is often affected by many exceptions, which could generate a number of preoccupations: What action should be taken in case of exceptions? Should we cancel the whole process for any exception? If not, what action should be canceled? For which type of exception? If you only need to cancel a certain number of transactions, how do you recognize them? And at the end of a batch processing, it is always important to know how many treatments have been canceled. How many have been registered successfully? How many have been ignored?

As you can see, we have not finished identifying questions that batch processing can raise, but we discover that this is already a great deal. Trying to build such a tool on your own may not only complicate your application but also introduce new bugs.

Understanding the Batch API

The Batch Applications API for the Java Platform 1.0 was developed to provide a solution to the different needs listed in the earlier bullet items. It targets both Java SE and Java EE applications and requires at least the 6th Version of JVM.

The features offered by this API can be summarized as follows:

- It offers the **Reader-Processor-Writer** pattern natively and gives you the ability to implement your own batch pattern. This allows you to choose the best pattern depending on the case.

- It gives the possibility of defining the behavior (skip, retry, rollback, and so on) of the batch processing for each type of error.

- It supports many step-level metrics such as: `rollbackCount`, `readSkipCount`, `writeSkipCount`, and so on for monitoring.

- It can be configured to run some processes in parallel and offer the possibility to use JTA or `RESOURCE_LOCAL` transaction mode.

To do this, the Batch Applications API for the Java Platform 1.0 is based on a solid architecture that can be outlined by the following diagram. A **Job** is managed by a `JobOperator` and has one or many steps, which can be either **chunk** or **batchlet**. During its lifecycle, information (metadata) about a job is stored in `JobRepository`, as shown in the following diagram:

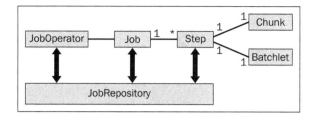

JobRepository

As we said earlier, `JobRepository` stores metadata about current and past running jobs. It can be accessed through `JobOperator`.

Job

A **Job** can be seen as an entity to encapsulate a unit of batch processing. It is made up of one or many steps, which must be configured within an XML file called a **Job configuration file** or **Job XML**. This file will contain job identification information and different steps that compose the job. The code that follows shows the skeleton of a Job XML file.

```
<job id="inscription-validator-Job" version="1.0"
  xmlns="http://xmlns.jcp.org/xml/ns/javaee">

  <step id="step1" >
    . . .
  </step>
  <step id="step2" >
    . . .
  </step>
</job>
```

The Job XML file is named with the convention `<name>.xml` (for example, `inscriptionJob.xml`) and should be stored under the `META-INF/batch-jobs` directory for portable application.

Step

A **Step** is an autonomous phase of a batch. It contains all the necessary information to define and control a piece of batch processing. A batch step is either a chunk or a batchlet (the two are mutually exclusive). The step of the following code is a chunk type step:

```
<job id="inscription-validator-Job" version="1.0"
  xmlns="http://xmlns.jcp.org/xml/ns/javaee">
  <step id="validate-notify" >
```

```
    <chunk>
      <reader ref="InscriptionReader" />
      <processor ref="InscriptionProcessor" />
      <writer ref="StudentNotifier" />
    </chunk>
  </step>
</job>
```

Chunk

A **chunk** is a type of step that implements the Reader-Processor-Writer pattern. It runs in the scope of a configurable transaction and can receive many configuration values. The following code is a more enhanced version of the **inscription-validator-Job** shown in the preceding code. In this listing, we have added a configuration to define the unit element that will be used in order to manage the commit behavior of the chunk (`checkpoint-policy="item"`), and a configuration to define the number of items (unit elements) to process before commit (`item-count="15"`). We have also specified the number of exceptions a step will skip if any configured exceptions that can be skipped are thrown by the chunk (`skip-limit="30"`).

The following code is an example of a chunk type step with some configuration:

```
<job id="inscription-validator-Job" version="1.0"
  xmlns="http://xmlns.jcp.org/xml/ns/javaee">
  <step id="validate-notify" >
    <chunk item-count="15" checkpoint-policy="item"
      skip-limit="30">
      <reader ref="InscriptionReader" />
      <processor ref="InscriptionProcessor" />
      <writer ref="StudentNotifier" />
    </chunk>
  </step>
</job>
```

The following code shows us what chunk batch artifact implementation looks like. The `InscriptionCheckpoint` allows you to know the line that is being processed. The source code of this section is a validation program that sends a message to the candidates to let them know if they have been accepted or not. At the end, it displays monitoring information in a web page. The processing is launched by the `ChunkStepBatchProcessing.java` Servlet.

The following code is a skeleton of chunk batch artifact implementations:

```java
public class InscriptionReader extends AbstractItemReader {
  @Override
  public Object readItem() throws Exception {
    //Read data and return the item
  }
}

public class InscriptionProcessor implements ItemProcessor{
  @Override
  public Object processItem(Object o) throws Exception {
    //Receive item from the reader, process and return the result
  }
}

public class StudentNotifier extends AbstractItemWriter {
  @Override
  public void writeItems(List<Object> items) throws Exception {
    //Receive items from the processor then write it out
  }
}
public class InscriptionCheckpoint implements Serializable {
  private int lineNumber;

  public void incrementLineNumber(){
    lineNumber++;
  }

  public int getLineNumber() {
    return lineNumber;
  }
}
```

Batchlet

A **batchlet** is a type of step to implement your own batch pattern. Unlike a chunk that performs tasks in three phases (reading, processing, and writing), a batchlet step is invoked once and returns an exit status at the end of processing. The following code shows us what a batchlet batch artifact implementation looks like. The source code of this section sends an information message to all students and displays some important information about the batch. The processing is launched by the `BatchletStepBatchProcessing.java` Servlet.

The following code is a skeleton of batchlet batch artifact implementation:

```
public class StudentInformation extends AbstractBatchlet{

  @Override
  public String process() throws Exception {
    // process
    return "COMPLETED";
  }
}
```

The batch.xml configuration file

The batch.xml file is an XML file that contains the batch artifacts of the batch application. It establishes a correspondence between the batch artifact implementation and the reference name that is used in the Job XML file. The batch.xml file must be stored in the META-INF directory for a portable application. The following code gives us the contents of the batch.xml file for the inscription-validator-Job Job shown in the preceding code.

The following code is an example of batch.xml:

```
<batch-artifacts xmlns="http://xmlns.jcp.org/xml/ns/javaee">
  <ref id="InscriptionReader"
  class="com.packt.ch02.batchprocessing.chunk.
    InscriptionReader" />
  <ref id="StudentNotifier"
  class="com.packt.ch02.batchprocessing.chunk.StudentNotifier" />
  <ref id="InscriptionProcessor"
  class="com.packt.ch02.batchprocessing.chunk.
    InscriptionProcessor" />
</batch-artifacts>
```

JobOperator

The JobOperator instance is accessible through the getJobOperator() method of the BatchRuntime class. It provides a set of operations to manage (start, stop, restart and so on) a job and access JobRepository (getJobNames, getJobInstances, getStepExecutions, and so on). The following code shows how to start the inscription-validator-Job Job shown earlier without any specific property. It is important to note that the inscriptionJob value that is specified in the JobOperator.start command is the name of the Job XML file (not the ID of the job). In the Servlet ChunkStepBatchProcessing, you will see how to retrieve the status and how to monitor information about batch processing from the JobOperator instance.

The following code is an example of code to start a Job:

```
JobOperator jobOperator = BatchRuntime.getJobOperator();
if(jobOperator != null)
  jobOperator.start("inscriptionJob", null);
```

Java API for JSON Processing 1.0

The Java API for JSON Processing 1.0 was developed under JSR 353. This section gives you only an overview of the API. The complete document specification (for more information) can be downloaded from `http://jcp.org/aboutJava/communityprocess/final/jsr353/index.html`.

What is JSON?

JavaScript Object Notation (JSON) is a lightweight data-interchange text format. It is based on a subset of JavaScript, but it is completely language independent. JSON format is often used for data exchanges between web client and web server or web service. But, it can be used whenever you need to store or transmit relatively small amounts of data that can easily be represented as a combination of name-value pairs.

JSON is built on two structures, which are: a collection of name-value pairs and an ordered list of values. These structures are made from three data types: `object`, `array`, and `value`.

Object

An **object** is an unordered set of `name:value` pairs within braces (`{}`). After each name, there is a colon (`:`) and the name-value pairs are separated by a comma (`,`). The name is `string` type while the type of the value can be `string`, `object` and so on The following text gives an example of a JSON object, which contains some information about a student:

```
{"name":"Malinda","gender":"F","birthday":"14/03/1976",
  "weight":78.5}
```

Array

An **array** is an ordered collection of values separated by a comma (`,`) within brackets (`[]`). The following text gives an example of a JSON array, which contains a list of students with their score in alphabetical order.

```
[{"name":"Amanda","score"=12.9},{"name":"Paolo","score"=14},
  {"name":"Zambo","score"=12.3}]
```

Value

A JSON **value** can be a `string` in double quotes, a `boolean` true or false, an `object`, an `array` or `null`.

Why JSON?

The **XML (Extensible Markup Language)** was released after the **SGML (Standardised Generalised Markup Language**, which was powerful and extensible but complex) and the **HTML (HyperText Markup Language**, a simple version of SGML focused on data presentation) to overcome the shortcomings of both languages. Its power, flexibility, and simplicity have favored its use in many applications for configuration management, storage, data transfer, and so on. With the advent of **AJAX** technologies, the use of XML was widespread in exchanges between browsers and web servers. But, it presented some limitations: XML documents are heavy in nature because of the duplication of information, loading, and handling of data can be complex and processing XML documents sometimes is browser dependent.

To provide a solution to these problems, the JSON format was developed as an alternative to XML. In fact, despite its portability and flexibility, JSON does not support namespaces, data access requires a knowledge of the document and until now, there is no **XSD** or **DTD** to validate the document's structure.

A simple comparison between XML and JSON data presentation is shown in the following table:

XML data presentation	JSON data presentation

`<student>`
`  <id>854963</id>`
`  <name>Louis`
`    Poyer</name>`
`  <weight>78.6</weight>`
`  <gender>M</gender>`
`  <contact>`
`    <address>Rue`
`      9632</address>`
`    <phone>985-761-0`
`      </phone>`
`  </contact>`
`</student>`
	`{"student": {`
	`  "id":"854963",`
	`  "name":"Louis`
	`    Poyer",`
	`  "weight":78.6,`
	`  "gender":"M",`
	`  "contact":[`
	`    {"address":"Rue`
	`      632"},`
	`    {"phone":`
	`      "985-761-0"} ]`
	`}`
	`}`

Java API for JSON processing

The Java API for JSON processing defines an API to process (`parse`, `generate`, `transform`, and `query`) JSON documents by using either the streaming API or the object model API.

The streaming API

The **streaming API** is for JSON as **StAX API** is for XML. In other words, the streaming API is an event-based JSON parsing. It parses a JSON file sequentially and fires an event whenever a it encounters a new tag in the stream (new value String, new start of objet, end of objet, new start of an array …). The example that follows shows us how to get contact information within the JSON data presented on the previous page.

Example of JSON processing using the streaming API:

```
public String getStudentContact(String jsonData) {
  JsonParser parser = Json.createParser
    (new StringReader(jsonData));
  Event event = null;
  boolean found = false;
  String information = "";

  //Advance to the contact key
  while (parser.hasNext()) {
    event = parser.next();
    if ((event == Event.KEY_NAME) &&
      "contact".equals(parser.getString())) {
        found = true;
        event = parser.next();
        break;
      }
  }

  if (!found) {
    return "contact information does not exist";
  }

  //get contact information
  while (event != Event.END_ARRAY) {
  switch (event) {
    case KEY_NAME:
      information += parser.getString() + " = ";
      break;
    case START_ARRAY: break;
```

```
         case END_ARRAY: break;
         case VALUE_FALSE: break;
         case VALUE_NULL: break;
         case VALUE_NUMBER:
           if (parser.isIntegralNumber()) {
             information += parser.getLong()+", ";
           } else {
             information += parser.getBigDecimal()+", ";
           }
           break;
         case VALUE_STRING:
           information += parser.getString()+", ";
           break;
         case VALUE_TRUE:
           information += " TRUE, ";
           break;
       }
       event = parser.next();
     }
     return information;
 }
```

The streaming API consists of five interfaces, one `enum` class, and two exceptions. All of them are contained in the `javax.json.stream` package. Among these interfaces, we have the `JsonParser` interface, which contains methods for step-by-step read-only access to JSON data, and the `JsonGenerator` interface, which provides methods to generate (write out) JSON step-by-step. Instances of these interfaces can be created respectively with `JsonParserFactory` and `JsonGeneratorFactory` factories. All events triggered by the streaming API are contained in the `JsonParser.Event enum` class.

It's recommended to use the streaming API to parse large JSON files because, unlike the object model API, it does not require loading the whole file before processing. This ensures good memory management.

The object model API

The object model API is for JSON as **DOM API** is for XML. This means that it represents a JSON document as a tree structure in memory before giving the possibility to navigate in or query the document. This API provides the most flexible way to parse a JSON document by giving a random access to any data it contains. But in return, it requires more memory. That is why it is not suitable for large documents.

The object model API consists of thirteen interfaces, one class, one enum class and one exception. All of them are packages in `javax.json`. Among interfaces, we have: `JsonArrayBuilder` and `JsonObjectBuilder` to build JSON arrays and JSON objects respectively from scratch; `JsonArray` to access the ordered values of a JSON array as a list and `JsonObject` to access the values of a JSON object as a Map and `JsonBuilderFactory` to create `JsonObjectBuilder` or `JsonArrayBuilder` instances; `JsonReader` to read JSON from an input source and `JsonReaderFactory` to create `JsonReader` instances; `JsonWriter` to write JSON to an output source, and `JsonWriterFactory` to create `JsonWriter` instances. The following code demonstrates how to create an object model from scratch and access data within it.

The following code is an example of JSON processing using the object model API:

```
JsonObject objModel = Json.createObjectBuilder()
.add("student",Json.createObjectBuilder()
  .add("id", "854963")
  .add("name", "Louis Poyer")
  .add("weight", 78.6)
  .add("gender","M")
  .add("contact",Json.createArrayBuilder()
    .add(Json.createObjectBuilder()
    .add("address","Rue 632"))
    .add(Json.createObjectBuilder()
    .add("phone","985-761-0")))
).build();

JsonObject student = objModel.getJsonObject("student");
String name = student.getString("name");
JsonArray contact = student.getJsonArray("contact");
String address = contact.getJsonObject(0).getString("address");
String phone = contact.getJsonObject(1).getString("phone"));
```

Java API for WebSocket 1.0

The Java API for WebSocket 1.0 was developed under JSR 356. This section just gives you an overview of the API. The complete document specification (for more information) can be downloaded from http://jcp.org/aboutJava/communityprocess/final/jsr356/index.html.

What is WebSocket?

Originally called **TCPConnection** in previous versions of the HTML5 specification, **WebSocket** is an independent protocol built over the **TCP (Transmission Control Protocol)**, which enables bidirectional and full-duplex communication between a client and a server.

To open a WebSocket connection in web application , the web client uses an HTTP request to ask the server to upgrade the connection to a WebSocket connection. If the server supports and accepts the WebSocket protocol connection request, it will still return a response through HTTP. From that moment, the communication is established and both parties can send and receive data by using only the WebSocket protocol.

Why WebSocket?

Today, many web applications (instant messaging, trading platforms, some e-commerce platforms, online gaming, and so on) require a real-time communication between a client (browser) and a server. If you do not know, the HTTP protocol is a stateless half-duplex protocol. This means that, to access new information and update a web page, the client must always open a connection to the server, send a request, wait for the server response, and then close the connection. Thus, in a real-time context, the client will frequently send requests to the server in order to detect the presence of new data and many request-responses will be made even when there is no new information.

To get around this problem, many solutions have been proposed. The most efficient was certainly long polling, which can be described like this: the client makes a request to the server; if there is data available, the server responds. Otherwise, it waits until there is new information before responding. After receiving the response, the client sends another request and so on. Although it seems good, this technique requires proprietary solutions (comet) and when data are frequently updated, the loop connection-request-response-disconnection may negatively impact the network.

WebSocket is not an HTTP-based technique, it is a protocol that provides a new and better way to overcome the shortcomings of the HTTP protocol in real-time communication between web client and web server/service.

The WebSocket API

The Java API for WebSocket 1.0 defines a standard API to build WebSocket-driven applications in the Java EE platform.

A WebSocket application consists of two types of components called endpoints: a client endpoint and a server endpoint. A client endpoint is the component that initiates a WebSocket connection, while a server endpoint is waiting for connections. With the Java API for WebSocket 1.0, both component types can be created either programmatically or declaratively by using annotations. In this chapter we will only see annotated endpoints in a small student chat room application.

Server endpoint

The following code demonstrates how to create a WebSocket endpoint that is able to accept client connections and send messages:

```
@ServerEndpoint("/chatserver")
public class ChatServerEndPoint {
  @OnOpen
  public void openConnection(Session session) throws Exception {
    //...
  }

  @OnMessage
  public void onMessage(Session session, String msg)
    throws Exception {
    //...
  }

  @OnClose
  public void closeConnection(Session session) throws Exception {
    //...
  }
}
```

The `@ServerEndpoint` annotation defines a server type endpoint and the path where it will be deployed. You will also notice that the API offers annotations to describe the method to be executed in each step of the endpoint lifecycle. The following table gives the list and the role of WebSocket endpoint lifecycle annotations.

The following table lists the WebSocket endpoint lifecycle annotations:

Annotation	Role
@OnOpen	Designates the method to be executed at the opening of a connection
@OnMessage	Designates the method to be executed when a message is received
@OnError	Designates the method to be executed in case of a connection error
@OnClose	Designates the method to be executed when the connection is closed

Any message sent by a WebSocket client is intercepted by the onMessage() method, which takes the client session and the message as parameters (for other parameters that can be taken, please see the specification). Messages can be sent synchronously with the method Session.getBasicRemote() or asynchronously with the method Session.getAsyncRemote(). Each of these methods is used to send messages of type: text, binary, object, ping, and pong frames. The following code demonstrates how to send a text message to all connected clients:

```
static Set<Session> users = Collections.synchronizedSet(new
HashSet());

  @OnOpen
  public void openConnection(Session session) throws Exception {
    users.add(session);
  }

  @OnMessage
  public void onMessage(Session session, String msg)
    throws Exception {
    for (Session s : users) {
      s.getBasicRemote().sendText(msg);
    }
  }
```

The session object contains a variable to store some user-specific information. The code that follows demonstrates how to communicate with many customers by giving the name of the person who sent the message each time:

```
//...
static Set<String> usersId = Collections.synchronizedSet(new
HashSet());
//...

@OnMessage
  public void onMessage(Session session, String msg)
    throws Exception {
    if (msg.startsWith("ID")) {//if it is a connection message
      String id = msg.split("-")[1];
      session.getUserProperties().put("id", id);
      //save the ID of the user
      usersId.add(id);
      //add the ID in the list of connected users
      Object[] obj1 = new Object[]
        {"wel","Welcome to the chat room "+id +"!"};
```

```
      String jsonString = getJsonObject(obj1);
      //json message transformation
      //send a welcome message to the new user
      session.getBasicRemote().sendText(jsonString);
      //send the list of connected users to all users
      Object[] obj2 = new Object[]{"users",usersId};
      jsonString = getJsonObject(obj2);
      for (Session s : users) {
        s.getBasicRemote().sendText(jsonString);
      }
    } else { //if it is a message to the chat room
      //get ID of the user who sends message
      String id = (String) session.getUserProperties().get("id");
      Object[] obj = new Object[]
      {"msg",id + ">>" + msg.split("-")[1]};
      String jsonString = getJsonObject(obj);//json transformation
      //sends the message to all connected users
      for (Session s : users) {
        s.getBasicRemote().sendText(jsonString);
      }
    }
  }
}
```

Client endpoint

Our client WebSocket endpoint is a `.jsp` web page (`websocketChatClient.jsp`) which is based on JavaScript code. As you can see, the client side has the same lifecycle methods and through the power of JSON, we can easily access and display messages sent by the server.

The following code is an example of a web client WebSocket endpoint:

```
//complete URI of the chat server endpoint
var clientUri = "ws://"+document.location.host
  +"/chapter02NewSpecifications/chatserver";
var wsocket;

//connection request when loading the web page
window.addEventListener("load", connect, false);

//Connection method
function connect() {
  wsocket = new WebSocket(clientUri);
  //binding of the websocket lifecycle methods
  wsocket.onmessage = onMessage;
```

```
        wsocket.onerror = onError;
    }

    function joinChatRoom() {//method to join the chat room
        wsocket.send("ID-" + txtMessage.value);
    }

    function sendMessage() {//method to send a message to the chat room
        wsocket.send("M-" + txtMessage.value);
    }

    function onMessage(event) {//method to perform incoming messages
      var parsedJSON = eval('(' + event.data + ')');
      if (parsedJSON.wel != null) {//if welcome message
        userState.innerHTML = parsedJSON.wel;
      }
      if (parsedJSON.msg != null) {//if chat room message
        userMessage.innerHTML += "\n"+parsedJSON.msg;
      }
      if (parsedJSON.users.length > 0) {//if new new connection user
        userId.innerHTML = "";
        for (i = 0; i < parsedJSON.users.length; i++) {
          userId.innerHTML += i + "-" + parsedJSON.users[i] + "\n";
        }
      }
    }
}
```

Summary

In this chapter we have tried to present the usefulness and implementation of the new specifications of Java EE 7. In the coming chapters, we will analyze the improvements that have been made to the specifications inherited from Java EE 6 and use the opportunity to show how to integrate new specifications with existing ones.

3

The Presentation Layer

In this chapter, we will review the improvements in the Java EE platform for the presentation layer. In concrete terms, we are going to talk about the following specifications:

- Servlet 3.1
- Expression Language 3.0
- JavaServer Faces 2.2

Servlet 3.1

The Servlet 3.1 Specification was developed under JSR 340. This section gives you only an overview of improvements in the API. The complete document specification (for more information) can be downloaded from `http://jcp.org/aboutJava/communityprocess/final/jsr340/index.html`.

What is a Servlet?

There was a time in computer science when we could not create dynamic web pages. At that time, users had access only to static web pages, such as in a newspaper. Among the many proposed solutions, the first Java solution was the **Servlet**, a revolutionary technology used to extend the capabilities of servers based on the request-response programming model. It enabled web servers to handle HTTP requests and dynamically generate web pages according to user parameters. Since then, technologies have advanced a lot in order to facilitate the development of web applications. However, the Servlet technology remains the most widely used Java solution for processing of HTTP requests/responses in the background.

That said, at the base of almost all Java frameworks dedicated to the HTTP protocol (JSF, Struts, Spring MVC, BIRT, web services solutions), you will find at least one Servlet (that is, you have `FacesServlet` in JSF, `ViewerServlet`, and the `BirtEngineServlet` for BIRT). You understand why this technology should attract our attention, because a change in the Servlet specification will have repercussions on a multitude of tools.

A login page with a Servlet

Concretely, a Servlet is a Java class that implements the Servlet interface directly or indirectly. The following code represents an example of a Servlet that returns a connection interface to the user and redirects it to another interface after validating its input:

```
@WebServlet(name = "connexionServlet", urlPatterns = {"/
connexionServlet"})
public class ConnexionServlet extends HttpServlet {

    Logger logger = Logger.getLogger(ConnexionServlet.class.
getName());

    protected void processRequest(HttpServletRequest request,
HttpServletResponse response) {
        response.setContentType("text/html;charset=UTF-8");
        try (PrintWriter out = response.getWriter();){
            out.println("<!DOCTYPE html>");
            out.println("<html>");
            out.println("<head>");
            out.println("<title>Online pre-registration site</
title>");
            out.println("</head>");
            out.println("<body>");
            out.write("        <form method=\"post\">");
            out.write("            <h4>Your name</h4>");
            out.write("            <input type=\"text\"
name=\"param1\" />");
            out.write("            <h4>Your password</h4>");
            out.write("            <input type=\"password\"
name=\"param2\" />");
            out.write("            <br/> <br/> <br/>");
            out.write("            <input type=\"submit\"
value=\"Sign it\"/>");
            out.write("            <input type=\"reset\"
value=\"Reset\" />");
            out.write("        </form>");
```

```
            out.println("</body>");
            out.println("</html>");

            String name = request.getParameter("param1");
            String password = request.getParameter("param2");

            String location = request.getContextPath();

            if("arnoldp".equals(name) && "123456".equals(password)){
                response.sendRedirect(location+"/
WelcomeServlet?name="+name);
                }else if((name != null) && (password != null))
                    response.sendRedirect(location+"/
ConnexionFailureServlet");

        } catch(IOException ex){
            logger.log(Level.SEVERE, null, ex);
        }
    }

    @Override
    protected void doGet(HttpServletRequest request,
HttpServletResponse response)
            throws ServletException, IOException {
        processRequest(request, response);
    }

    @Override
    protected void doPost(HttpServletRequest request,
HttpServletResponse response)
            throws ServletException, IOException {
        processRequest(request, response);
    }
}
```

As you can see, our `ConnexionServlet` class extends `javax.servlet.http.HttpServlet`; this is an abstract class that implements the `Servlet` interface. It defines the lifecycle methods (`doGet` and `doPost`) of the `Servlet` object that allows us to handle HTTP service requests and send back a response. To access the page generated by this Servlet, you must enter an URL similar to this one: `http://localhost:8080/chapter03PresentationLayer/connexionServlet`. Here, `connexionServlet` is the name given in the `@WebServlet` annotation. On this page, you will have the **Sign it** button displayed by using the following instruction:

```
    out.write("                <input type=\"submit\"  value=\"Sign it\"/>");
```

A click on this button generates an HTTP request that will cause execution of the `pro cessRequest(HttpServletRequest request, HttpServletResponse response)` method. Based on the results of the `connexion` parameters validation, you will be redirected to the error page or home page. In the case of a redirect to the home page, we will add to the URL a parameter containing the name of the user in order to adapt the greeting. The URL of the homepage is the following:

```
http://localhost:8080/chapter03PresentationLayer/
WelcomeServlet?name=arnoldp
```

To access the `name` parameter, we execute the instruction: `out.println("<h1>Welcome Mr " + request.getParameter("name")+ "</h1>");` in the `WelcomeServlet` Servlet.

Latest improvements of Servlet 3.1 in action

Following Servlet 3.0, which was focused on ease of development, pluggability, asynchronous processing, and security enhancements, Servlet 3.1 has brought a number of clarifications to features of the previous version and some changes; the main ones are: non blocking I/O API and protocol upgrade processing.

Non blocking I/O API

The non blocking I/O API piggybacks on the asynchronous request processing and the upgrade processing to improve the scalability of the Web Container. Indeed, the introduction of asynchronous processing in Servlet 3.0 has made it possible to reduce waiting time between requests by enabling the thread responsible for processing the client's requests and delegating to other threads the execution of heavy processes in order to be ready to accept a new request. But, because of the traditional way to collect data input/output with a `while` loop (see the following code), the main thread responsible for request processing can be blocked due to pending data. For example, when you send a large amount of data to a very powerful server across a network, the time taken for data collection will be inversely proportional to the bandwidth of the network. The smaller the bandwidth, the more time the server will take to do the job.

```
public class TraditionnalIOProcessing extends HttpServlet {

    Logger logger = Logger.getLogger(TraditionnalIOProcessing.class.
getName());

    protected void doGet(HttpServletRequest request,
HttpServletResponse response) {
        try (ServletInputStream input = request.getInputStream();
```

```
                    FileOutputStream outputStream = new
    FileOutputStream("MyFile");) {

            byte b[] = new byte[3072];
            int data = input.read(b);

            while (data != -1) {
                outputStream.write(b);
                data = input.read(b);
            }
        } catch (IOException ex) {
            logger.log(Level.SEVERE, null, ex);
        }
    }
}
```

To solve this problem, two listeners (`ReadListener` and `WriteListener`) have been added to the Java EE platform and new APIs were also introduced into `ServletInputStream` and `ServletOutputStream`.

The following table describes the new listeners for the non blocking I/O API:

Listener	Callbacks	Description
ReadListener	void onDataAvailable()	This method is called whenever data is available to read without blocking
	void onAllDataRead()	This method is called when all the data of `ServletRequest` has been read
	void onError(Throwable t)	This method is called when an error or exception occurs during request processing
WriteListener	void onWritePossible()	This method is called whenever it is possible to write data without blocking
	void onError(Throwable t)	This method is called when an error or exception occurs during response processing

The table that follows describes the new APIs for the non blocking I/O API:

Class	Method	Description
ServletInputStream	void setReadListener(Readlistener ln)	This associates Readlistener with the current ServletInputStream
	boolean isFinished()	This returns true when all the data of ServletInputStream has been read
	boolean isReady()	This returns true if data can be read without blocking
ServletOutputStream	boolean isReady()	This returns true if data can be written successfully to ServletOutputStream
	void setWriteListener(WriteListener ln)	This associates WriteListener with the current ServletOutputStream

By using the non blocking I/O API, the doGet(HttpServletRequest request, HttpServletResponse response) method of the TraditionnalIOProcessing class shown earlier may be transformed to the doGet(HttpServletRequest request, HttpServletResponse response) method represented in the following code. As you can see, the data reception has been delegated to a listener (ReadListenerImpl), which will be notified whenever a new package is available. This prevents the server from being blocked while waiting for new packages.

```
protected void doGet(HttpServletRequest request, HttpServletResponse
response) {
    try (ServletInputStream input = request.getInputStream();
            FileOutputStream outputStream = new
FileOutputStream("MyFile");) {
        AsyncContext context = request.startAsync();
        input.setReadListener(new ReadListenerImpl(context,
input,outputStream));
    }catch (IOException ex) {
        logger.log(Level.SEVERE, null, ex);
    }
}
```

The implementation of `ReadListenerImpl` used in the preceding code snippet is as follows:

```java
public class ReadListenerImpl implements ReadListener {

    AsyncContext context;
    ServletInputStream input;
    FileOutputStream outputStream;

    public ReadListenerImpl(AsyncContext c, ServletInputStream i,
FileOutputStream f) {
        this.context = c;
        this.input = i;
        outputStream = f;
    }

    @Override
    public void onDataAvailable() throws IOException {
        byte b[] = new byte[3072];
        int data = input.read(b);
        while (input.isReady() && data != -1) {
            outputStream.write(b);
            data = input.read(b);
        }
    }

    @Override
    public void onAllDataRead() throws IOException {
        System.out.println("onAllDataRead");
    }

    @Override
    public void onError(Throwable t) {
        System.out.println("onError : " + t.getMessage());
    }
}
```

Protocol upgrade processing

Protocol upgrade processing is a mechanism that was introduced in HTTP 1.1 to provide the possibility of switching from HTTP protocol to another (one that is completely different). A concrete example of protocol upgrade processing usage is the migration from HTTP protocol to the WebSocket protocol where the client begins by sending a request for WebSocket to the server. The client request is sent via HTTP and if the server accepts the connection request, it will still respond through HTTP. From this moment, every other communication will be through the established WebSocket channel. Support for this mechanism in the Servlet 3.1 Specification was done by adding the `upgrade` method to `HttpServletRequest` and two new interfaces: `javax.servlet.http.HttpUpgradeHandler` and `javax.servlet.http.WebConnection`.

The following table shows a description of protocol upgrade methods, interfaces, and classes:

Class/Interface	Method	Description
`HttpServletRequest`	`HttpUpgradeHandler upgrade(Class handler)`	This method starts the upgrade processing, instantiates, and returns the handler class that implements the `HttpUpgradeHandler` interface.
`HttpUpgradeHandler`	`void init(WebConnection wc)`	This method is called when the upgrade operation is accepted by the Servlet. It takes a `WebConnection` object to allow the protocol handler have access to the input/output streams.
	`void destroy()`	This method is called when the client disconnects.
`WebConnection`	`ServletInputStream getInputStream()`	This method gives access to the input stream of the connection.
	`ServletOutputStream getOutputStream()`	This method gives access to the output stream of the connection.

The two blocks of code that follow show us how the new method and new interfaces can be used in order to accept a given client protocol upgrade request.

The following is an example of an upgrading request:

```
protected void processRequest(HttpServletRequest request,
HttpServletResponse response)
            throws ServletException, IOException {
        response.setContentType("text/html;charset=UTF-8");
    try (PrintWriter out = response.getWriter();){
            System.out.println("protocol : "+request.
getHeader("Upgrade"));
        if ("CYPHER".equals(request.getHeader("Upgrade"))) {
            response.setStatus(101);
            response.setHeader("Upgrade", "CYPHER");
            response.setHeader("Connection", "Upgrade");
```

```
                CypherUpgradeHandler cHandler = request.
upgrade(CypherUpgradeHandler.class);
        } else {
            out.println("The "+request.getHeader("Upgrade")+" protocol
is not supported");
        }
    }
}
```

The following is an example of upgrade handler class implementation:

```
public class CypherUpgradeHandler implements HttpUpgradeHandler{

    Logger logger = Logger.getLogger(CypherUpgradeHandler.class.
getName());
    public void init(WebConnection wc) {
        ServletInputStream input = null;
        ServletOutputStream output = null;
        try {
            System.out.println("A client just logged in");
            input = wc.getInputStream();
            // use input stream
            output = wc.getOutputStream();
            //use output stream
        } catch (IOException ex) {
            logger.log(Level.SEVERE, null, ex);
        }
    }

    public void destroy() {
        System.out.println("A client just logged out");
    }
}
```

Expression Language 3.0

The Expression Language 3.0 Specification was developed under JSR 341. This section gives you only an overview of improvement in the API. The complete document specification (for more information) can be downloaded from http://jcp.org/aboutJava/communityprocess/final/jsr341/index.html.

What is Expression Language?

Expression Language (EL) is a language used to access and manipulate data in your JSP or JSF web pages. It provides a simple way to:

- Read/write data from/to JavaBean component properties
- Invoke static and public methods
- Perform arithmetic, relational, logical, and conditional operations

An EL expression looks like `${expr}` or `#{expr}`. The former syntax is often used for immediate evaluation while the latter is used for deferred evaluation. The following code demonstrates how to access a JSF bean property from a JSF page and how to perform an operation between two integers using EL expressions:

```
<h:form>
   <h:outputText
     id="beanProperty"
     value="Bean property value : #{studentBean.identity}" />
   <br/>
   <h:outputText
       id="operator"
       value="operator : 3 + 12 = #{3 + 12}"  />
</h:form>
```

The latest improvements of EL 3.0 in action

EL was first designed for **JSP Standard Tag Library** (**JSTL**), before being associated with the JSP Specification and then to the JSF Specification. Since both specifications had different needs at the onset, each specification used a variant of the EL. The advent of JSP 2.1 EL led to unification of the EL used in JSP and JSF pages; this gave birth to a dedicated specification document for EL, although EL was always dependent on the same JSR as JSP. Version 3.0 is the first to be developed in a separate JSR: JSR 341. This new specification comes with many changes; the most important are: an API for standalone environments, lambda expressions, collection object support, string concatenation operator, assignment operator, semi-colon operator, and static fields and methods.

API for standalone environments

Since EL 3.0, it is now possible to handle EL in a standalone environment. For this purpose, it provides the `ELProcessor` class, which allows direct evaluation of EL expressions and makes easier the definition of functions, variables, and local repository beans. The following code demonstrates how the `ELProcessor` class can be used in standalone environment. The present case is the content of a Servlet, but you can do the same in a Java SE application.

```
ELProcessor el = new ELProcessor();

//Simple EL evaluation
  out.println("<h1>'Welcome to the site!' : "
             + "" + el.eval("'Welcome to the site!'") + "</h1>");
//Definition of local repository bean
el.defineBean("student", new StudentBean());
//Direct evaluation of EL expression
out.println("<h1>" + el.eval("'The id of : '+=student.lastName+=' "
             + "is : '+=student.identity") + "</h1>");
//Function definition
el.defineFunction("doub", "hex", "java.lang.Double","toHexString");
//Access to a function defined
out.println("<h1> The hexadecimal of 29 is : "
             + el.eval("doub:hex(29)") + "</h1>");
```

Always in the context of the API for standalone environments, EL 3.0 has added the `ELManager` class to provide lower-level APIs that enable the management of the EL parsing and evaluation environment. With this class, you can import classes or add your own resolver to `ELProcessor`.

Lambda expressions

A lambda expression is an anonymous function that consists of one or more parameters in brackets (if there are several), the lambda operator (->), and the body of the lambda expression. The expression: x-> x * x, is a lambda expression used to determine the square of a number. Basically, lambda expressions save you from having to create a whole class for a single method or to declare a method for a very simple operation that will be used once. So, they can help to write more readable and maintainable code.

A lambda expression can take many forms, as follows:

- It may involve a number of parameters and can be invoked immediately. The expression: `((x,y,z)->x+y*z)(3,2,4)`, returns 11.

- It can be associated with an identifier and invoked later. The expression: `diff = (x,y)-> x-y; diff(10,3)`, returns 7.

- It can be passed as an argument to a method or nested within another lambda expression. The expression: `diff=(x,y)->(x-y);diff(10,[ 2,6,4,5].stream().filter(s->s < 4).max().get())`, returns 8.

Collection object support

The support of collection objects in the EL 3.0 Specification is done in two ways: the construction of collection objects and implementation of operations that will be used to manipulate them.

Collection object construction

Concerning the creation of a collection, EL allow us to create objects of type `java.lang.util.Set`, `java.lang.util.List`, and `java.lang.util.Map` dynamically by using an expression or literals.

The different types of object construction are as follows:

- Set object construction:

  The construction of `Set` collection type results in an instance of `Set <Object>` and it is done according to the following syntax:

  `SetCollectionObject = '{'elements '}'`

  Here, `elements` has the form `(expression (',' expression)* )?`

  For example: `{1, 2, 3, 4, 5}, {'one','two','three','four'}, {1.3, 2, 3,{4.9, 5.1}}`

- List object construction:

  The construction of `List` collection type results in an instance of `List<Object>` and it is done according to the following syntax:

  `ListCollectionObject = '['elements']'`

  Here, `elements` has the form `(expression (',' expression)* )?`

  For example: `[one, 'two', ['three', 'four'],five], [1, 2, 3, [4,5]]`

- Map object construction:

  The construction of `Map` object type results in an instance of `Map<Object>` and it is done according to the following syntax:

  ```
  MapCollectionObject = '{' MapElements '}'
  ```

  Here, `MapElements` has the form `(MapElement (',' MapElement)* )?` and `MapElement` the form `expression ':' expression`

  For example: `{1:'one', 2:'two', 3:'three', 4:'four'}`

Collection operations

The second aspect of the collection support in EL 3.0 concerns collection operations. For this aspect, the specification only defines the syntax and behavior of a standard set of collection operations to be implemented with `ELResolvers`. It has the advantage of allowing developers to modify the default behavior by providing their own `ELResolvers`.

Execution of a collection operation is done through a stream pipeline which is made up of:

- A `stream` object that represents the source of a pipeline; it is obtained from the `stream()` method of the collection or array. In the case of a map, the collection view of the map can be use as the source.
- Zero or more intermediate `stream` methods that return a `stream` object.
- A terminal operation, which is a `stream` method that returns nothing.

The following code demonstrates the construction of a pipeline by giving an example of collection operations:

```
public class ELTestMain {
    static ELProcessor el = new ELProcessor();

    public static void main(String[] args) {
        List l = new ArrayList();
        l.add(1); l.add(8); l.add(7); l.add(14); l.add(2);
        el.defineBean("list", l);

        out.println("Evaluation of " + l + " is : " +
el.eval("list"));
        out.println("The ordering of: " + l + " is : "
                + el.eval("list.stream().sorted().toList()"));
```

```
        out.println("List of number < 7 : "
                + el.eval("list.stream().filter(s->s <
7).toList()"));
        out.println("The sum of : " + l + " is : "
                + el.eval("list.stream().sum()"));
    }
}
```

String concatenation operator (+=)

The += operator returns the concatenation of operands located on either side of the operator. For example, 1 += 2 returns 12 while 1 + 2 returns 3. To welcome a new connected student to our website we only need to locate the following expression somewhere in a web page:

#{'Welcome' += studentBean.lastName}.

Assignment operator (=)

The A = B expression assigns the value of B to A. To make this possible, A must be a writable property. The assignment operator (=) can be used to change the value of a property. For example, the #{studentBean.identity = '96312547'} expression assigns the value 96312547 to property studentBean.identity.

 The assignment operator returns a value and it is right-associative. The expression a = b = 8 * 3 is the same as a = (b = 8 * 3).

Semi-colon operator (;)

The semi-colon operator can be used like the comma operator in C or C++. When two expressions exp1 and exp2 are separated by a semi-colon operator, the first expression is evaluated before the second, and it is the result of the second expression that is returned. The first expression may be an intermediate operation, such as incrementation, whose result will be used in the last expression.

The expression: a = 6+1; a*2 returns 14.

Static fields and methods

With EL 3.0, it is now possible to directly access static fields and methods of a Java class by using the syntax `MyClass.field` or `MyClass.method`, where `MyClass` is the name of the class that contains the static variable or method. The code that follows demonstrates how to access the `MIN_VALUE` field of the `Integer` class and how to parse the String `'2'` to int by using the static `parseInt` method of the `Integer` class:

```
ELProcessor el = new ELProcessor();
//static variable access
out.println("<h1> The value of Integer.MIN_VALUE : "
                + el.eval("Integer.MIN_VALUE") + "</h1>");
//static method access
out.println("<h1> The value of Integer.parseInt('2') : "
                + el.eval("Integer.parseInt('2')") + "</h1>");
```

JavaServer Faces 2.2

The JavaServer Faces 2.2 Specification was developed under JSR 344. This section gives you only an overview of improvements in the API. The complete document specification (for more information) can be downloaded from `http://jcp.org/aboutJava/communityprocess/final/jsr344/index.html`.

What is JavaServer Faces?

JavaServer Faces (JSF) is a component-based architecture with a set of standard UI widgets and helper tags (`convertDateTime`, `inputText`, `buttons`, `table`, `converter`, `inputFile`, `inputSecret`, `selectOneRadio`). It was released after the Servlet and JSP Specification in order to facilitate the development and maintenance of component-oriented web applications. In this light, it offers developers the ability to:

- Create web applications that meet the design pattern of MVC (Model-View-Controller). This design pattern allows a clear separation of the presentation layer from the other layers and facilitates the maintenance of the whole application.
- Create different types of components (widgets, validators, and so on).

- Reuse and customize multiple components provided by the specification according to need.

- Bind Java components to different views and manipulate them easily by using **Expression Language** (EL).

- Generate web pages in different formats (HTML, WML, and so on) through render kits.

- Intercept the various events that occur on a form and manage the lifecycle of Java components according to the request scope.

To make this possible, the lifecycle of JSF applications includes six phases (restore view phase, apply request values, process validations, update model values, invoke application, and render response), each of which manages a specific aspect while processing the form instead of just managing requests/responses, as is the case with Servlets.

An identification page with JSF

The following code shows an example of a JSF page to enter personal information, such as first name and nationality. It also contains components for selection lists and checkboxes. As you can see, it is not necessary to be a geek to make a good job. To manage the navigation after validation of parameters, we use the `action` attribute of the `commandButton` component that expects a return value from the method `onclickValidateListener`. The web page that follows displays relative to the value returned and is defined in the `faces-config.xml` file of the web application.

```xml
<?xml version='1.0' encoding='UTF-8' ?>
<!DOCTYPE html PUBLIC "-//W3C//DTD XHTML 1.0 Transitional//EN"
    "http://www.w3.org/TR/xhtml1/DTD/xhtml1-transitional.dtd">
<html xmlns="http://www.w3.org/1999/xhtml"
    xmlns:h="http://xmlns.jcp.org/jsf/html"
    xmlns:f="http://xmlns.jcp.org/jsf/core">
    <h:head>
        <title>Online pre-registration site</title>
    </h:head>
    <h:body>
        <f:view>
            <h:form >
                <dir align="center" >
                    <h:panelGrid columns="2" style="border: solid
blue">
                        <h:outputText value="First name   : " />
                        <h:inputText value="#{studentBean.firstName}"
/>
```

```
                    <h:outputText value="Last name : " />
                    <h:inputSecret value="#{studentBean.lastName}"
/>
                    <h:outputText value="Birth date: " />
                    <h:inputSecret value="#{studentBean.
birthDate}" />
                    <h:outputText value="Birth place : " />
                    <h:inputSecret value="#{studentBean.
birthPlace}" />
                    <h:outputText value="Nationality : " />
                    <h:selectOneMenu value="#{studentBean.
nationality}">
                        <f:selectItems value="#{studentBean.
nationalities}" />
                    </h:selectOneMenu>
                    <h:outputText value="Gender : " />
                    <h:selectOneRadio value="#{studentBean.
gender}">
                        <f:selectItem itemValue="M"
itemLabel="Male" />
                        <f:selectItem itemValue="F"
itemLabel="Female" />
                    </h:selectOneRadio>
                    <h:outputText value="Language : " />
                    <h:selectOneMenu value="#{studentBean.
language}">
                        <f:selectItems value="#{studentBean.
languages}" />
                    </h:selectOneMenu>
                    <dir align="right">
                        <h:panelGroup>
                            <h:commandButton value="Validate"
action="#{studentBean.onclickValidateListener}" />
                            <h:commandButton value="Cancel"
actionListener="#{studentBean.onclickCancelListener}"  />
                        </h:panelGroup>
                    </dir>
                </h:panelGrid>
            </dir>
        </h:form>
    </f:view>
  </h:body>
</html>
```

The latest improvements of JSF 2.2 in action

Because of the great improvements provided in HTML5, a priority of JSF 2.2 was to incorporate new features of the language; but this is not the only big change. Besides the integration of HTML5, the JSF 2.2 Specification comes with Resource Library Contracts, which announce multitemplate features, Faces Flow, and Stateless Views.

HTML5-friendly markup

As we saw earlier, JSF is a component-based architecture. This justifies the fact that the creation of relatively complex user interface features is done by the development of JavaServer Faces components. These components are processed on the server side before delivering the right content to the browser. Although this approach saves the developer from the complexity of HTML, scripts, and other resources involved in each component, you have to know that the creation of a component is not always easy and the generated code is not always the lightest or most optimal.

The advent of HTML5 has greatly simplified the development of web applications with the introduction of new features, new elements, and new attributes. To avoid JSF component developers from reinventing the wheel, JSF 2.2 has integrated support of markup through two major concepts: pass-through attributes and pass-through elements.

Pass-through attributes

During the generation of web pages that will be sent to the browser, the attributes for each JSF component are interpreted and validated by the `UIComponent` or Renderer. Unlike adding HTML5 attributes into all JSF components so that they can be validated by the `UIComponent` or Renderer, pass-through attributes give developers the ability to list a set of attributes that will be passed straight through to the browser without being interpreted by the `UIComponent` or Renderer. This can be done with three different approaches:

- By introducing the namespace `xmlns:pta="http://xmlns.jcp.org/jsf/passthrough"`; this will be used to prefix all of the component attributes that must be copied without interpretation into the web page intended for the browser (see `Pass through attributes 1` in the code that follows)

- By nesting the `<f:passThroughAttribute>` tag within a `UIComponent` tag for a single attribute (see `Pass through attributes 2` in the following code)

- By nesting the `<f:passThroughAttributes>` tag within a `UIComponent` tag for an EL value that is evaluated to `Map<String, Object>` (see `Pass through attributes 3` in the code that follows)

```
<!-- namespace -->
<html   ...
        xmlns:pta="http://xmlns.jcp.org/jsf/passthrough">

<h:form>
    <!-- Pass through attributes 1 -->
    <h:inputText pta:type="image" pta:src="img_submit.gif"
                 value="image1" pta:width="58" pta:height="58" />

    <!-- Pass through attributes 2 -->
    <h:inputText value="image2" >
        <f:passThroughAttribute name="type" value="image" />
        <f:passThroughAttribute name="src" value="img_submit.gif"
/>
        <f:passThroughAttribute name="width" value="68" />
        <f:passThroughAttribute name="height" value="68" />
    </h:inputText>

    <!-- Pass through attributes 3 -->
    <h:inputText value="image3" >
        <f:passThroughAttributes
           value="#{html5Bean.mapOfParameters}" />
    </h:inputText>
</h:form>
```

Pass-through elements

In contrast to pass-through attributes that allow you to pass HTML attributes to the browser without interpretation, pass-through elements allow you to use the HTML tag as a JSF component. This gives you the opportunity to enrich the HTML tag with JSF features and take advantage of the JSF component lifecycle. To make this possible, the framework will establish a correspondence between the HTML markup specified by the developer, which is rendered to the browser, and an equivalent JSF component for server-side processing.

To use pass-through elements in a given HTML tag, you must prefix at least one of its attributes with the short name assigned to the `http://xmlns.jcp.org/jsf` namespace.

The following code snippet shows how to use pass-through elements:

```
<!-- namespace -->
<html ...
      xmlns:pte="http://xmlns.jcp.org/jsf"">

<h:form>
    <!-- Pass through element -->
    <input type="submit" value="myButton"
     pte:actionListener="#{html5Bean.submitListener}"/>
</h:form>
```

Resource Library Contracts

The Resource Library Contracts provide a JSF mechanism for applying templates to different parts of your web application. This feature announces a major change: the ability to download a look and feel (theme) and apply it to your account or website by using a button or management console, as in Joomla!.

For now, the Resource Library Contracts enable you to group resources (template files, JavaScript files, style sheets, and images) of your various templates in the contracts folder of your web application. To improve the maintainability of your application, resources for each template can be grouped into a subfolder called contract. The following code demonstrates a web application with three templates stored in three different contracts: template1, template2, and template3:

```
src/main/webapp
    WEB-INF/
    contracts/
        template1/
            header.xhtml
            footer.xhtml
            style.css
            logo.png
            scripts.js
        template2/
            header.xhtml
            footer.xhtml
            style.css
            logo.png
            scripts.js
        Template3/
            header.xhtml
            footer.xhtml
            style.css
```

```
        logo.png
        scripts.js

    index.xhtml
    ...
```

In addition to the deployment in the `contracts` folder, your templates can be packaged in a JAR file; in this case, they must be stored in the `META-INF/contracts` folder of the JAR which will be deployed in the `WEB-INF/lib` folder of your application.

Once defined, templates must be referenced within an application's `faces-config.xml` file, with the `resource-library-contracts` element. The configurations of the following request mean that `template1` is applied to pages whose URLs respect the pattern `/templatepages/*`. And for other pages, the `template2` will be applied.

```
<resource-library-contracts>
    <contract-mapping>
        <url-pattern>/templatepages/*</url-pattern>
        <contracts>template1</contracts>
    </contract-mapping>
    <contract-mapping>
        <url-pattern>*</url-pattern>
        <contracts>template2</contracts>
    </contract-mapping>
</resource-library-contracts>
```

The following code snippet shows us what the header of `template1` looks like. It contains only a picture to be displayed in the header. You can add text, style, and color if you want.

```
<?xml version='1.0' encoding='UTF-8' ?>
<!DOCTYPE html>
<html xmlns="http://www.w3.org/1999/xhtml"
      xmlns:h="http://xmlns.jcp.org/jsf/html"
      xmlns:f="http://xmlns.jcp.org/jsf/core"
      xmlns:ui="http://xmlns.jcp.org/jsf/facelets">
    <h:head>
        <title>Resource Library Contracts</title>
    </h:head>
    <h:body>
      <ui:insert name="header" >
        <img src="image.jpg" width="400" height="50" alt="Header
image"/>
      </ui:insert>
    </h:body>
</html>
```

The following code demonstrates how a template can be used in a web page:

```
<f:view>
    <h:form>
        <h:panelGrid border="1" columns="3" >
            <f:facet name="header">
                <ui:composition template="/header.xhtml">

                </ui:composition>
            </f:facet>
            <f:facet name="footer">
                <ui:composition template="/footer.xhtml">

                </ui:composition>
            </f:facet>
        </h:panelGrid>
    </h:form>
</f:view>
```

Faces Flow

Faces Flow is used to define and perform processes that are split over several forms. If we take, for example, the case of online registration, the registration form can be split over several pages, each representing a step. In our case we have: the acceptance conditions, entering identification information, contact information, medical information, school information, and finally the validation. To implement this type of application with previous versions of JSF, it was necessary to use beans with session scope and declare hard links between pages that formed the flow. This reduces the usability of the flow in another application and does not give the possibility to open the same flow in many windows.

A flow is made up of an entry called the starting point, an exit point called a return node and zero, or many other nodes. A node can be a JSF page (ViewNode), a navigation decision (SwitchNode), an application logic invocation (MethodCallNode), a call to another flow (FlowCallNode), or a return to the calling flow (ReturnNode).

A flow can be configured either with an XML configuration file or programmatically. It can be packaged in a JAR file or folder. The following example demonstrates how to implement an online preregistration website with Faces Flow (our flow is configured with an XML configuration file; for program configuration, please consult the Java EE 7 tutorial.)

In the case of a flow packaged in a folder, the following conventions are followed by default:

- The package folder of the flow has the same name as the flow
- The starting node of the flow has the same name as the flow
- All pages of the flow are assumed to be in the same folder except the exit points
- For a flow that is configured with an XML configuration file, the configuration file is a `faces-config` whose name is `<name_of_flow>-flow.xml`

According to the rule we have just presented, the web application that the tree is showing contains a flow named `inscriptionFlow` with six views. This flow is configured in `inscriptionFlow-flow.xml` and its starting node is `inscriptionFlow.xhtml`.

```
webapp
  WEB-INF
  inscriptionFlow
      inscriptionFlow-flow.xml
  inscriptionFlow.xhtml
  inscriptionFlow1.xhtml
  inscriptionFlow2.xhtml
  inscriptionFlow3.xhtml
  inscriptionFlow4.xhtml
  inscriptionFlow5.xhtml
  ...
    index.xhtml
```

In the configuration file, we must define the ID of the flow and the ID of exit points. The following code shows the contents of the file `inscriptionFlow-flow.xml`:

```xml
<?xml version='1.0' encoding='UTF-8'?>
<faces-config version="2.2"
    xmlns="http://xmlns.jcp.org/xml/ns/javaee"
    xmlns:xsi="http://www.w3.org/2001/XMLSchema-instance"
    xsi:schemaLocation="http://xmlns.jcp.org/xml/ns/javaee
http://xmlns.jcp.org/xml/ns/javaee/web-facesconfig_2_2.xsd">

    <flow-definition id="inscriptionFlow">
        <flow-return id="inscriptionFlowExit">
            <from-outcome>#{inscriptionFlowBean.exitValue}</from-outcome>
        </flow-return>
    </flow-definition>
</faces-config>
```

Navigation between different views can be done through the `action` attribute of the tag that will actuate the display of the next view. In this attribute you put the name of the page to which you want to go after the current page. The following code shows the contents of the `inscriptionFlow1` view. This view corresponds to the input form for personal information; it contains a field for entering the name, a button to go to the next view (`inscriptionFlow2`), and a button to return to the previous view (`inscriptionFlow`).

```
<!-- inscriptionFlow1 view -->
<f:view>
<h:form>
    <h1>Identification information</h1>
    <p>Name : <h:inputText id="name"
            value="#{inscriptionFlowBean.name}" /></p>

   <p><h:commandButton value="Next" action="inscriptionFlow2" /></p>
   <p><h:commandButton value="Back" action="inscriptionFlow" /></p>
</h:form>
</f:view>
```

To end a flow, just pass to the `action` attribute of the dedicated tag for this action the ID of the exit point defined in the configuration file (`inscriptionFlowExit`). And to save data between different views, you must use a Flow-Scoped Managed Bean. The following code shows the skeleton of the `inscriptionFlowBean` managed bean that we use in our inscription flow:

```
@Named
@FlowScoped(value="inscriptionFlow")
public class InscriptionFlowBean {
    //...
}
If all settings have been made, you can call your inscriptionFlow  in
the start page with a button as follows:
<h:commandButton id="start" value="Registration"
                                action="inscriptionFlow">
   <f:attribute name="toFlowDocumentId" value=""/>
</h:commandButton>
```

Stateless views

JSF 2.2 did not only add new widgets, it also improved memory usage. Prior to Version 2.0 of the specification, the whole component tree was saved and restored whenever there was any change in the view. This degraded system performance and stuffed the memory. With Version 2.0, the specification has introduced the partial state saving mechanism. This mechanism consists of saving only the state that has changed after the creation of the component tree and reduces the amount of data to be saved. In the same light, JSF 2.2 offers us the possibility to define stateless views. As the name suggests, no data about the `UIComponent` state of the view's components will be saved.

To transform a simple view into a stateless view, you just need to specify `true` as the value of the transient attribute of the `f:view` tag (see the following code).

```
<h:head>
    <title>Facelet Title</title>
</h:head>
<h:body>
    <f:view transient="true">
        <h:form>
            Hello from Facelets
        </h:form>
    </f:view>
</h:body>
```

Summary

In this chapter, we discussed the specifications related to data presentation that have been improved in Java EE 7. These are: Servlet, Expression Language, and the JSF Specification. Each presentation was followed by an analysis of the various improvements made and a small example to show how these new features can be implemented. In the next chapter, we will talk about Java APIs used to communicate with databases, which will lead us to another chapter that focuses on putting together all of the APIs that we have seen.

4

The Java Persistence API

This chapter deals with the improvements in APIs for communicating with data sources. Although Java is object oriented, it is designed to handle data of relational models as objects, which might pose a serious problem because the two concepts are not theoretically compatible. In addition to introducing you to the world of object-relational mapping, this chapter will show you how to manipulate (create, delete, search, or edit) the data of relational models as objects transparently and transactional. Topics covered in this chapter are:

- Java Persistence API 2.1
- Java Transaction API 1.2

Java Persistence API 2.1

The Java Persistence API 2.1 Specification was developed under **JSR-338**. This section just gives you an overview of the improvements in the API. The complete document specification (for more information) can be downloaded from `http://jcp.org/aboutJava/communityprocess/final/jsr338/index.html`.

JPA (Java Persistence API)

JPA (**Java Persistence API**) is a Java specification that aims to define the standard features of **ORMs** (**Object-Relational Mappings**). However, JPA is not a product but a set of interfaces that require implementations. The most well-known implementations are as follows: **Hibernate, Toplink, OpenJPA,** and **EclipseLink,** which is the reference implementation.

Briefly, we can say that an ORM is an API used to establish a correspondence between the object model and a relational database. It gives you the ability to handle the data of your database as if they were objects, without too much worry about the physical schema.

JPA in action

JPA is based on the concept of entities, in order to make object-relational mapping possible. An entity is a simple Java class (like **POJO**) with `@Entity` annotation (or XML equivalent) whose name is by default associated with the table having the same name in the database. In addition to the `@Entity` annotation, an entity class must have at least one primary key equivalent attribute that is designated with the `@Id` annotation (or XML equivalent). For the other attributes of the entity, the provider associates each of them to the column having the same name in the table, as shown in the following screenshot:

```
@Entity
public class Student {
    @Id
    private String id;
    private String firstname;
    private String lastname;
    @Temporal(TemporalType.DATE)
    private Date birthdate;
    private String phone;
    private String email;

    /*
      getter and setter methods
    */
}
```

student
ID VARCHAR(15)
FIRSTNAME VARCHAR(30)
LASTNAME VARCHAR(30)
BIRTHDATE DATE
PHONE VARCHAR(10)
EMAIL VARCHAR(60)
Indexes

The parameters that indicate the database that will be associated to a set of entities must be defined in the persistence unit within the `persistence.xml` file of your application.

The following code is an example of the persistence unit of a Java SE Application:

```
<?xml version="1.0" encoding="UTF-8"?>
<persistence version="2.1"
  xmlns="http://xmlns.jcp.org/xml/ns/persistence"
  xmlns:xsi="http://www.w3.org/2001/XMLSchema-instance"
  xsi:schemaLocation="http://xmlns.jcp.org/xml/ns/persistence
  http://xmlns.jcp.org/xml/ns/persistence/persistence_2_1.xsd">
  <persistence-unit name="chapter04PU"
    transaction-type="RESOURCE_LOCAL">
    <provider>org.eclipse.persistence.jpa.PersistenceProvider
      </provider>
    <class>com.packt.ch04.entities.Student</class>
    <properties>
      <property name="javax.persistence.jdbc.url"
        value="jdbc:derby://localhost:1527/ONLINEREGISTRATION"/>
      <property name="javax.persistence.jdbc.password"
        value="userapp"/>
```

```
          <property name="javax.persistence.jdbc.driver"
            value="org.apache.derby.jdbc.ClientDriver"/>
          <property name="javax.persistence.jdbc.user"
            value="userapp"/>
        </properties>
      </persistence-unit>
    </persistence>
```

Concerning the manipulation of entities, JPA offers through the `EntityManager` interface a set of methods to create, read, update, and delete the data (see the following table).

The following table presents some methods for manipulating the entities:

Method	Description
`void persist(Object o)`	This is used to save the entity passed as a parameter.
`T merge(T t)`	This allows you to merge the entity passed as a parameter with the persistence context. It returns a managed version of the entity to be merged.
`void remove(Object o)`	This allows you to delete the entity passed as parameter in the database.
`T find(Class<T> type, Object o)`	This allows you to search for an entity using its identifier.
`void detach(Object o)`	This allows you to detach an entity from the persistence context so that the changes will not be saved

The following code demonstrates how to save, read, update, and delete the data using JPA in a Java SE application:

```
public static void main( String[] args ) {
  EntityManagerFactory emf =
    Persistence.createEntityManagerFactory("chapter04PU");
  EntityManager em = emf.createEntityManager();
  //create entity manager

  Student student = createStudent();

  em.getTransaction().begin();//begin transaction
  em.persist(student);//save the student
  em.getTransaction().commit(); // commit transaction
```

```
Student std = em.find(Student.class, student.getId());
//find student

System.out.println("ID : "+std.getId()+",
  last name : "+std.getLastname());
em.getTransaction().begin();//begin transaction
std.setLastname("NGANBEL");//Update student's last name
em.getTransaction().commit(); // commit transaction

std = em.find(Student.class, student.getId());//find student
System.out.println("ID : "+std.getId()+",
  last name : "+std.getLastname());

em.getTransaction().begin();//begin transaction
em.remove(std);//remove student
em.getTransaction().commit(); // commit transaction
}
```

The latest improvements of JPA 2.1 in action

Since its last version (JPA 2.0), the JPA Specification has had many enhancements.
The most important enhancements are in the following features: persistence
context synchronization, Entities, **JPQL**, **Criteria API**, and **Data Definition
Language** (DDL) generation.

Persistence context synchronization

Before JPA 2.1, the container-managed persistence context was automatically joined
to the current transaction, and any update made to the persistence context was
propagated to the underlying resource manager. With the new specification, it is
now possible to have a persistence context that will not be automatically enlisted in
any JTA transaction. This can be done by simply creating a container-managed entity
manager of synchronization type SynchronizationType.UNSYNCHRONIZED as shown
in the following code.

Creation and enlistment of a SynchronizationType.UNSYNCHRONIZED
persistence context:

```
@Stateless
@LocalBean
public class MySessionBean {

  /* Creation of an entity manager for
   * unsynchronized persistence context
```

```
*/
@PersistenceContext(synchronization = SynchronizationType.
UNSYNCHRONIZED)
EntityManager em;

public void useUnsynchronizedEntityManager(){
    //enlisting of an unsynchronized persistence context
    em.joinTransaction();
    //...
}
}
```

In the preceding code, you will notice that we called the `EntityManager.`
`joinTransaction()` method; this is justified by the fact that a persistence context
of type `SynchronizationType.UNSYNCHRONIZED` is enlisted in a JTA transaction
only after calling the `EntityManager.joinTransaction()` method, and after a
commit or rollback, the `SynchronizationType.UNSYNCHRONIZED` persistence context
will be dissociated from the transaction to which it was enlisted. You need to call
the `EntityManager.joinTransaction()` method again to enlist the dissociated
persistence context.

Entity

An entity listener is a simple Java class (not an entity), which allows you to define the
lifecycle callback methods that can be invoked for the lifecycle events of one or many
entities. The JPA 2.1 Specification adds to these classes the support of **CDI injection**
and the ability to define `@PostConstruct` and `@PreDestroy` lifecycle callback
methods. These methods are respectively called after the dependency injections and
before the destruction of the entity listener. The following code presents an entity
listener that has the post construct and pre destroy methods with an **EJB injection**.
It is followed by code that shows how to associate an entity listener to an entity.

```
public class LogEntityListener {
  @EJB
  BeanLoggerLocal beanLogger;

  @PrePersist
  public void prePersistCallback(Object entity){
    beanLogger.logInformation(entity);
  }

  @PostConstruct
  public void init(){
    System.out.println("Dependency injected in
      LogEntityListener");
```

```
  }

  @PreDestroy
  public void destroy(){
    System.out.println("LogEntityListener will be destroy");
  }
}

@Entity
@EntityListeners(LogEntityListener.class)
public class Student implements Serializable {
  //
}
```

New annotations

JPA 2.1 added an annotation (@Index) to create indexes on tables when a schema is generated from entities and an annotation (@ForeignKey) to designate foreign keys of a table.

The @Index annotation has one mandatory parameter (columnList) to list the columns that make up the index with different sort orders. It also has two optional parameters: the name parameter, which allows you to change the default name of the index, and the unique parameter to set the index as unique or not unique. In parallel, @Index annotation was added as a part of Table, SecondaryTable, CollectionTable, JoinTable, and TableGenerator annotations.

The @ForeignKey can be used as element of JoinColumn, JoinColumns, MapKeyJoinColumn, MapKeyJoinColumns, PrimaryKeyJoinColumn, PrimaryKeyJoinColumns, CollectionTable, JoinTable, SecondaryTable, and AssociationOverride annotations to either define or modify the foreign key constraints on a table. It takes three parameters: name, value for the constraint, and the definition of the foreign key. The three parameters are optional.

An example of an entity with a foreign key and indexed columns is shown in the following code:

```
@Entity
@Table(indexes = @Index(columnList = "name ASC, id DESC"))
public class MyEntity implements Serializable {
  @Id
  private Long id;
  private String name;
  @JoinColumn(foreignKey = @ForeignKey(name = "FK"))
  private Student student;
  //...
}
```

Entity graphs

When we talk about an entity graph, we have to keep in mind a data structure involving several related entities. With the previous version of JPA, the efficient loading of data of an entity was essentially managed through the fetch setting. The consequence was that it was necessary to set the fetch attribute of some annotations before compiling the application (or before deployment in the case of XML configuration) in order to request that an entity attribute be loaded **eagerly** (when entity is loaded) or **lazily** (when data is needed). Through entity graphs, you can now override or change the fetch setting at runtime.

An entity graph can be defined statically by using a vast NamedEntityGraph, NamedEntityGraphs, NamedSubgraph, and NamedAttributeNode annotations, or dynamically through EntityGraph, subgraph, and AttributeNode interfaces.

Static or named entity graphs

The @NamedEntityGraph annotation is used to define an entity graph that can be used at runtime when executing queries or using the find() method. The following code shows an example of the definition of a named entity graph with one field: students.

```
@Entity
@NamedEntityGraph(name="includeThis",
  attributeNodes={@NamedAttributeNode("students")})
public class Department implements Serializable {
  private static final long serialVersionUID = 1L;
  @Id
  @Basic(optional = false)
  private String id;
  private String name;
  private Integer nbrlevel;
  private String phone;
  @OneToMany(mappedBy = "depart",fetch = FetchType.LAZY)
  private List<Student> students;

  /*getter and setter*/
}
```

Once defined, we need to retrieve our named entity graph using the getEntityGraph() method of EntityManager in order to use it as a property when searching with the find method or as a **query hint** with a query. After executing the following code, you will notice that in the first search, the students attribute will not be loaded while in the second search it will be.

The following code is an example of using a named entity graph:

```
EntityManager em = emf.createEntityManager();
//create entity manager
PersistenceUnitUtil pUtil = emf.getPersistenceUnitUtil();

Department depart = (Department) em.createQuery
  ("Select e from Department e")
.getResultList().get(0);
System.out.println("students Was loaded ? "+pUtil.isLoaded
  (depart, "students"));

EntityGraph includeThis = em.getEntityGraph("includeThis");
depart = (Department) em.createQuery("Select e from Department e")
.setHint("javax.persistence.fetchgraph", includeThis)
.getResultList().get(0);
System.out.println("students Was loaded ? "+pUtil.isLoaded(depart,
  "students"));
```

Dynamic entity graphs

Entity graphs can also be defined at runtime. To do this, we must use the
createEntityGraph() method of the entity manager and not getEntityGraph() as
with the named entity graphs. Once defined, the **dynamic entity graph** is associated
with the find() method or a query in the same way as a named entity graph as
shown in the following code.

The following code is an example of using a dynamic entity graph:

```
EntityManager em = emf.createEntityManager();
//create entity manager
PersistenceUnitUtil pUtil = emf.getPersistenceUnitUtil();

Department depart = (Department) em.createQuery(
  "Select e from Department e")
.getResultList().get(0);
System.out.println("students Was loaded ? " + pUtil.isLoaded(depart,
"students"));

EntityGraph includeThis = em.createEntityGraph(Department.class);
includeThis.addAttributeNodes("students");

depart = (Department) em.createQuery("Select e from Department e")
.setHint("javax.persistence.fetchgraph", includeThis)
.getResultList().get(0);
System.out.println("students Was loaded ? " +
  pUtil.isLoaded(depart, "students"));
```

JPQL

JPQL (**Java Persistence Query Language**) is an object-oriented SQL-like query language. It is platform independent and allows you to access your data through entities instead of manipulating the physical structure of your database. The following code demonstrates how to query for all registered students whose ID is greater than 123.

The following code is an example of a JPQL query:

```
String queryString = "SELECT a FROM Student a WHERE a.id > 123";
Query query = em.createQuery(queryString);
System.out.println("result : "+query.getResultList());
```

Despite its power and its vastness, the JPQL continues to receive significant improvements. In JPA 2.1, it has among other enhancements integrated support for stored procedures, added new reserved identifiers, and the support for creation of named queries at runtime.

Support for stored procedures

JPA 2.1 now allows you to execute stored procedures. Through the various API that it offers, you can define and execute named stored procedures or dynamically stored procedures.

The following script is an example of a script to create a stored procedure in MySQL:

```
DELIMITER $$
CREATE
  PROCEDURE `ONLINEREGISTRATION`.`getStudentsName`()
  BEGIN
    SELECT ID,LASTNAME FROM STUDENT ORDER BY LASTNAME ASC;
  END$$
DELIMITER ;
```

The following code demonstrates how to execute the stored procedure getStudentsName we just created:

```
EntityManagerFactory emf = Persistence.createEntityManagerFactory("chapter04PUM");
EntityManager em = emf.createEntityManager();
//create entity manager
StoredProcedureQuery spQuery = em.createStoredProcedureQuery
  ("getStudentsName",Student.class);
List<Student> results = spQuery.getResultList();
for(Student std : results)
  System.out.println(std.getLastname());
```

New reserved identifiers

The JQPL has introduced the following new keywords:

- ON: This keyword allows us to make explicit joins as in SQL with the ON condition. Before, joins were made with the liaison attributes between the two entities, which required minimal configuration. The following code demonstrates the use of ON:

```
String queryString = "SELECT a FROM Student a "+
  " JOIN Department b ON a.departId = b.id";
Query query = em.createQuery(queryString);
System.out.println("result : "+query.getResultList());
```

- FUNCTION: This keyword allows you to invoke functions in your queries other than those originally intended by JPQL (such SUBSTRING, LENGTH, ABS, TRIM, and so on). With this keyword, you can use a database function or functions that you have defined yourself. The following query gives us the list of students born in July by using the month() method of **derby database** in order to extract the month from a birth date:

```
String queryString= "SELECT a FROM Student a "+
  " WHERE FUNCTION('MONTH',a.birthdate) = 7 ";
Query query = em.createQuery(queryString);
System.out.println("result : "+query.getResultList());
```

- TREAT: This keyword allows you to do the **downcasting** of an entity in order to obtain a subclass state. It is used in the FROM and WHERE clauses. In the following code, the entity Appuser inherits from the entity Person; with the keyword TREAT we can put conditions on attributes that are not contained in the base entity (Person).

```
//Entity downcasting
String queryString = "SELECT  a FROM Person a "
  +" WHERE TYPE(a) = Appuser AND "
  +" TREAT(a AS Appuser).userLogin = 'adwiner'";
Query query = em.createQuery(queryString);
System.out.println("result : "+query.getResultList());
```

Support for creating named queries at runtime

Before JPA 2.1, named queries were defined statically as metadata before compiling the program. Through the addNamedQuery method that was added to the EntityManagerFactory interface, you can now create a named query at runtime as shown in the following code:

```
EntityManagerFactory emf =
  Persistence.createEntityManagerFactory("chapter04PU");
```

```
EntityManager em = emf.createEntityManager();

Query query = em.createQuery("SELECT a FROM Student a");
emf.addNamedQuery("runtimeNamedQuery", query);

System.out.println("result :
  "+em.createNamedQuery("runtimeNamedQuery").getResultList());
```

The Criteria API

JPA since Version 2.0 offers two options for defining queries on entities. The first option is the JPQL which is a query language based on SQL. The second option is the Criteria API where a query is constructed essentially with Java objects, as shown in the following code:

```
EntityManagerFactory emf =
  Persistence.createEntityManagerFactory("chapter04PU");
EntityManager em = emf.createEntityManager();
//create entity manager
//criteria builder declaration
CriteriaBuilder cb = em.getCriteriaBuilder();
//declaration of the object that will be returned by the query
CriteriaQuery<Student> cq = cb.createQuery(Student.class);
//Declaration of the entity to which the request is made
Root<Student> student = cq.from(Student.class);
//Query construction
cq.select(student).where(cb.greaterThan(student.<String>
  get("id"), "123"));
TypedQuery<Student> tq = em.createQuery(cq);
//execution of the query
System.out.println("result : "+tq.getResultList());

//JPQL equivalent query
SELECT a FROM Student a WHERE a.id > 123
```

Given that the two solutions do not evolve at the same rate, the major changes in the Criteria API are support for bulk update/delete and new reserved identifiers.

Support for bulk update/delete

The bulk update and delete in the Criteria API are respectively constructed with `javax.persistence.criteria.CriteriaUpdate` and `javax.persistence.criteria.CriteriaDelete` interfaces. The following code demonstrates how to update a lot of information with just one Criteria API request:

```
//bulk update
CriteriaUpdate cUpdate = cb.createCriteriaUpdate(Student.class);
Root root = cUpdate.from(Student.class);
```

```
cUpdate.set(root.get("departId"), "GT")
  .where(cb.equal(root.get("departId"), "GI"));
Query q = em.createQuery(cUpdate);

em.getTransaction().begin();//begin transaction
int num = q.executeUpdate();
em.getTransaction().commit();//commit transaction
System.out.println("number of update : "+num);
//JPQL equivalent query
UPDATE Student a SET a.departId = 'GT' WHERE a.departId = 'GI'
```

Support for new reserved identifiers

Just like the JPQL, the Criteria API incorporates the possibility of making downcasts and defines joins using ON conditions. To do that, overloaded `treat()` methods have been added to the `javax.persistence.criteria.CriteriaBuilder` interface for downcasting, while `on()` and `getOn()` methods have been added to some interfaces (such as `Join`, `ListJoin`, `SetJoin`, `MapJoin`, `CollectionJoin`, and `Fetch`) of the `javax.persistence.criteria` package for joins with ON conditions. The following query is equivalent to the JPQL downcasting shown in the preceding code:

```
//Downcasting
CriteriaQuery<Person> cqp = cb.createQuery(Person.class);
Root<Person> person = cqp.from(Person.class);
cqp.select(person).where(cb.equal(person.type(),Appuser.class),
  cb.equal(cb.treat(person, Appuser.class).get("userLogin"),
  "adwiner"));
TypedQuery<Person> tqp = em.createQuery(cqp);
System.out.println("result : " + tqp.getResultList());
```

DDL generation

Since the previous version of the JPA Specification, it is possible to create or drop and create tables. However, the support for this feature was not required and the specification document made us understand that the use of this feature could reduce application portability. Well, with JPA 2.1, the **DDL** (**Data Definition Language**) generation was not only standardized but has been expanded and is now required.

In this case, new properties have been added. You have for example the following properties:

- `javax.persistence.schema-generation.database.action`: This defines the action (none, create, drop-and-create, or drop) that should be taken by the provider.

- `javax.persistence.schema-generation.create-source`: This defines the source (entities, specific scripts, or both) to be used by the provider in the case of a DDL generation.

- `javax.persistence.schema-generation.drop-source`: This defines the source (entities, specific scripts, or both) to be used by the provider in the case of drop table.

- `javax.persistence.schema-generation.connection`: This defines the **JDBC** connection parameters to use for the DDL schema generation in order to take into account the management of privileges in some databases such as Oracle. This parameter was thought of for Java EE environments.

The following persistence unit provides an example of configuration to generate tables at the creation of `EntityManagerFactory`. This generation will be based on entities' information (metadata) and it will take place if and only if the tables to be created do not exist, because we defined create instead of drop-and-create for the action of the provider.

```
<persistence-unit name="chapter04PUM" transaction-type="RESOURCE_
LOCAL">
  <provider>org.eclipse.persistence.jpa.PersistenceProvider
    </provider>
  <class>com.packt.ch04.entities.Department</class>
  <class>com.packt.ch04.entities.Person</class>
  <class>com.packt.ch04.entities.Student</class>
  <properties>
    <property name="javax.persistence.jdbc.url"
      value="jdbc:mysql://localhost:3306/onlineregistration"/>
    <property name="javax.persistence.jdbc.password"
      value="onlineapp"/>
    <property name="javax.persistence.jdbc.driver"
      value="com.mysql.jdbc.Driver"/>
    <property name="javax.persistence.jdbc.user" value="root"/>
    <property name="javax.persistence.
      schema-generation.database.action" value="create"/>
    <property name="javax.persistence.
      schema-generation.create-source" value="metadata"/>
  </properties>
</persistence-unit>
```

Another aspect of this standardization is the addition of a new method (`Persistence.generateSchema()`), which provides more opportunity for the generation. Before (in JPA 2.0), the DDL generation was done at the creation of the entity manager. Henceforth, you can generate your tables before, during, or after the creation of the `EntityManagerFactory`.

The following code demonstrates how to generate tables regardless of the creation of the EntityManagerFactory:

```
Map props = new HashMap();
props.put("javax.persistence.
   schema-generation.database.action", "create");
props.put("javax.persistence.
   schema-generation.create-source", "metadata");
Persistence.generateSchema("chapter04PUM", props);
```

The following code demonstrates another way to generate the tables at the creation of the EntityManagerFactory:

```
Map props = new HashMap();
props.put("javax.persistence.
   schema-generation.database.action", "create");
props.put("javax.persistence.
   schema-generation.create-source", "metadata");
EntityManagerFactory emf = Persistence.
   createEntityManagerFactory("chapter04PUM", props);
```

Java Transaction API 1.2

The Java Transaction API 1.2 Specification was developed under JSR 907. This section just gives you an overview of improvement in the API. The complete document specification (for more information) can be downloaded from http://jcp.org/aboutJava/communityprocess/mrel/jsr907/index2.html.

The Java Transaction API

The **Java Transaction API (JTA)** is a standard Java API for managing transactions on one or more resources (distributed transactions) in server environments. It consist of three main APIs: javax.transaction.UserTransaction interface used by applications for explicit transaction demarcation, javax. transaction.TransactionManager interface used by application servers to demarcate transactions implicitly on behalf of the application, and javax. transaction.xa.XAResource, which is a Java mapping of the standard XA interface for distributed transaction processing.

JTA in action

As we said, JTA transactions are used in Java EE environments. In order to enable this transaction type, the `transaction-type` attribute of the persistence unit should be set to `JTA` instead of `RESOURCE_LOCAL` and the data source (if there is one), should be defined within the `<jta-datasource>` element. The following code gives an example of a persistence unit to manage transactions using JTA:

```
<?xml version="1.0" encoding="UTF-8"?>
<persistence version="2.1"
  xmlns="http://xmlns.jcp.org/xml/ns/persistence"
  xmlns:xsi="http://www.w3.org/2001/XMLSchema-instance"
  xsi:schemaLocation="http://xmlns.jcp.org/xml/ns/persistence
  http://xmlns.jcp.org/xml/ns/persistence/persistence_2_1.xsd">

  <persistence-unit name="chapter04PU" transaction-type="JTA">
    <provider>org.eclipse.persistence.jpa.PersistenceProvider
      </provider>
    <jta-data-source>onlineRegDataSource</jta-data-source>
  </persistence-unit>

</persistence>
```

After declaring a `JTA` transaction type persistence unit, the developer can either leave the transaction management to the server (by default, the container considers a method as a transaction) or take control and define the transaction boundaries programmatically.

The following code is an example of a container-managed transaction:

```
@Stateless
public class StudentServiceCMT {

  @PersistenceContext
  EntityManager em;

  public void createStudent(){
    Student student = new Student();
    student.setBirthdate(new Date());
    student.setDepartid("GI");
    student.setId(""+ new Date().getTime());
    student.setFirstname("CMT - FIRST NAME");
    student.setLastname("CMT - Last name");

    em.persist(student);
  }
}
```

The following code is an example of bean-managed transaction:

```
@Stateless
@TransactionManagement(TransactionManagementType.BEAN)
public class StudentServiceBMT {

  @PersistenceContext
  EntityManager em;

  @Resource
  UserTransaction userTx;

  public void createStudent() throws Exception {
    try {
      userTx.begin();//begin transaction

      Student student = new Student();
      student.setBirthdate(new Date());
      student.setDepartid("GI");
      student.setId(""+ new Date().getTime());
      student.setFirstname("BMT - FIRST NAME");
      student.setLastname("BMT - Last name");

      em.persist(student);

      userTx.commit(); // commit transaction
      } catch (Exception ex) {
      userTx.rollback();//rollback transaction
      throw ex;
    }
  }
}
```

Innovations introduced by JTA 1.2

Unlike the JPA Specification, JTA has known only a few improvements that can be summarized in the following lines. First we have the addition of two new annotations. The first is `javax.transaction.Transactional`, which provides the possibility to demarcate transactions declaratively on CDI-managed beans or classes defined as managed beans by the Java EE Specification. The second annotation added is the `javax.transaction.TransactionScoped` annotation, which provides the possibility to define beans whose lifecycle is identical with the current transaction. The JTA API also added one exception class `javax.transaction.TransactionalException`.

Summary

In this chapter we have, with examples, presented and analyzed the improvements provided by two APIs whose major objective is to facilitate interaction with your data base. The first presented was JPA API, which gives you the ability to create, read, update, and delete data from a database by using Java objects. The second was JTA API, which is an API designed for transparent management of transactions in one or more data sources.

In the next chapter, we'll talk about **EJBs** and we will make a small example, which will consist of putting together most of the APIs that we have studied.

5
The Business Layer

Here we will begin with a presentation of improvements in the business layer and then, in a small project, we will try to put together some of the specifications seen previously. The topics to be covered include:

- Enterprise JavaBeans 3.2
- Putting all Java EE 7 specifications together

Enterprise JavaBeans 3.2

The Enterprise JavaBeans 3.2 Specification was developed under JSR 345. This section just gives you an overview of improvements in the API. The complete document specification (for more information) can be downloaded from `http://jcp.org/aboutJava/communityprocess/final/jsr345/index.html`.

The business layer of an application is the part of the application that is located between the presentation layer and data access layer. The following diagram presents a simplified Java EE architecture. As you can see, the business layer acts as a bridge between the data access and the presentation layer.

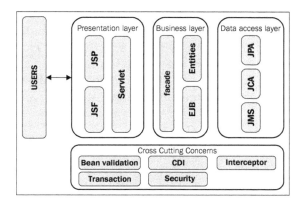

It implements business logic of the application. To do so, it can use some specifications such as Bean Validation for data validation, CDI for context and dependency injection, interceptors to intercept processing, and so on. As this layer can be located anywhere in the network and is expected to serve more than one user, it needs a minimum of non functional services such as security, transaction, concurrency, and remote access management. With EJBs, the Java EE platform provides to developers the possibility to implement this layer without worrying about different non functional services that are necessarily required.

In general, this specification does not initiate any new major feature. It continues the work started by the last version, making optional the implementation of certain features that became obsolete and adds slight modification to others.

Pruning some features

After the pruning process introduced by Java EE 6 from the perspective of removing obsolete features, support for some features has been made optional in Java EE 7 platform, and their description was moved to another document called *EJB 3.2 Optional Features for Evaluation*. The features involved in this movement are:

- EJB 2.1 and earlier Entity Bean Component Contract for Container-Managed Persistence
- EJB 2.1 and earlier Entity Bean Component Contract for Bean-Managed Persistence
- Client View of EJB 2.1 and earlier Entity Bean
- EJB QL: Query Language for Container-Managed Persistence Query Methods
- JAX-RPC-based Web Service Endpoints
- JAX-RPC Web Service Client View

The latest improvements in EJB 3.2

For those who have had to use EJB 3.0 and EJB 3.1, you will notice that EJB 3.2 has brought, in fact, only minor changes to the specification. However, some improvements cannot be overlooked since they improve the testability of applications, simplify the development of session beans or Message-Driven Beans, and improve control over the management of the transaction and passivation of stateful beans.

Session bean enhancement

A session bean is a type of EJB that allows us to implement business logic accessible to local, remote, or Web Service Client View. There are three types of session beans: **stateless** for processing without states, **stateful** for processes that require the preservation of states between different calls of methods, and **singleton** for sharing a single instance of an object between different clients.

The following code shows an example of a stateless session bean to save an entity in the database:

```
@Stateless
public class ExampleOfSessionBean  {

    @PersistenceContext EntityManager em;

    public void persistEntity(Object entity){
        em.persist(entity);
    }
}
```

Talking about improvements of session beans, we first note two changes in stateful session beans: the ability to execute life-cycle callback interceptor methods in a user-defined transaction context and the ability to manually disable passivation of stateful session beans.

It is possible to define a process that must be executed according to the lifecycle of an EJB bean (post-construct, pre-destroy). Due to the @TransactionAttribute annotation, you can perform processes related to the database during these phases and control how they impact your system. The following code retrieves an entity after being initialized and ensures that all changes made to the persistence context are sent to the database at the time of destruction of the bean. As you can see in the following code, TransactionAttributeType of init() method is NOT_SUPPORTED; this means that the retrieved entity will not be included in the persistence context and any changes made to it will not be saved in the database:

```
@Stateful
public class StatefulBeanNewFeatures  {

    @PersistenceContext(type= PersistenceContextType.EXTENDED)
    EntityManager em;

    @TransactionAttribute(TransactionAttributeType.NOT_SUPPORTED)
    @PostConstruct
    public void init(){
```

```
        entity = em.find(...);
    }

    @TransactionAttribute(TransactionAttributeType.REQUIRES_NEW)
    @PreDestroy
    public void destroy(){
        em.flush();
    }
}
```

The following code demonstrates how to control passivation of the stateful bean. Usually, the session beans are removed from memory to be stored on the disk after a certain time of inactivity. This process requires data to be serialized, but during serialization all transient variables are skipped and restored to the default value of their data type, which is `null` for object, zero for `int`, and so on. To prevent the loss of this type of data, you can simply disable the passivation of stateful session beans by passing the `false` value to the `passivationCapable` attribute of the `@Stateful` annotation.

```
@Stateful(passivationCapable = false)
public class StatefulBeanNewFeatures {
    //...
}
```

For the sake of simplicity, EJB 3.2 has relaxed the rules to define the default local or remote business interface of a session bean. The following code shows how a simple interface can be considered as local or remote depending on the case:

```
//In this example, yellow and green are local interfaces
public interface yellow { ... }
public interface green { ... }

@Stateless
public class Color implements yellow, green { ... }

//In this example, yellow and green are local interfaces
public interface yellow { ... }
public interface green { ... }


@Local
@Stateless
public class Color implements yellow, green { ... }

//In this example, yellow and green are remote interfaces
public interface yellow { ... }
```

```
public interface green { ... }


@Remote
@Stateless
public class Color implements yellow, green { ... }

//In this example, only the yellow interface is exposed as a remote
interface
@Remote
public interface yellow { ... }
public interface green { ... }


@Stateless
public class Color implements yellow, green { ... }

//In this example, only the yellow interface is exposed as a remote
interface
public interface yellow { ... }
public interface green { ... }

@Remote(yellow.class)
@Stateless
public class Color implements yellow, green { ... }
```

EJB Lite improvements

Before EJB 3.1, the implementation of a Java EE application required the use of a full Java EE server with more than twenty specifications. This could be heavy enough for applications that only need some specification (as if you were asked to take a hammer to kill a fly). To adapt Java EE to this situation, JCP (Java Community Process) introduced the concept of profile and EJB Lite. Specifically, EJB Lite is a subset of EJBs, grouping essential capabilities for local transactional and secured processing. With this concept, it has become possible to make unit tests of an EJB application without using the Java EE server and it is also possible to use EJBs in web applications or Java SE effectively.

In addition to the features already present in EJB 3.1, the EJB 3.2 Specification has added support for local asynchronous session bean invocations and non persistent EJB Timer Service. This enriches the embeddable `EJBContainer`, web profiles, and augments the number of testable features in an embeddable `EJBContainer`. The following code shows an EJB packaged in a WAR archive that contains two methods. The `asynchronousMethod()` is an asynchronous method that allows you to compare the time gap between the end of a method call on the client side and the end of execution of the method on the server side. The `nonPersistentEJBTimerService()` method demonstrates how to define a non persistent EJB Timer Service that will be executed every minute while the hour is one o'clock:

```
@Stateless
public class EjbLiteSessionBean {

    @Asynchronous
    public void asynchronousMethod(){
        try{
            System.out.println("EjbLiteSessionBean - start : "+new
Date());
            Thread.sleep(1000*10);
            System.out.println("EjbLiteSessionBean - end : "+new
Date());
        }catch(Exception ex){
            ex.printStackTrace();
        }
    }

    @Schedule(persistent = false, minute = "*", hour = "1")
    public void nonPersistentEJBTimerService(){
        System.out.println("nonPersistentEJBTimerService method
executed");
    }
}
```

Changes made to the TimerService API

The EJB 3.2 Specification enhanced the `TimerService` API with a new method called `getAllTimers()`. This method gives you the ability to access all active timers in an EJB module. The following code demonstrates how to create different types of timers, access their information, and cancel them; it makes use of the `getAllTimers()` method:

```
@Stateless
public class ChangesInTimerAPI implements ChangesInTimerAPILocal {

    @Resource
    TimerService timerService;
```

```
    public void createTimer(){
        //create a programmatic timer
        long initialDuration = 1000*5;
        long intervalDuration = 1000*60;
        String timerInfo = "PROGRAMMATIC TIMER";
        timerService.createTimer(initialDuration, intervalDuration,
timerInfo);
    }

    @Timeout
    public void timerMethodForProgrammaticTimer(){
        System.out.println("ChangesInTimerAPI - programmatic timer :
"+new Date());
    }

    @Schedule(info = "AUTOMATIC TIMER", hour = "*", minute = "*")
    public void automaticTimer(){
        System.out.println("ChangesInTimerAPI - automatic timer :
"+new Date());
    }

    public void getListOfAllTimers(){
        Collection<Timer> alltimers = timerService.getAllTimers();

        for(Timer timer : alltimers){
            System.out.println("The next time out : "+timer.
getNextTimeout()+", "
                    + " timer info : "+timer.getInfo());
            timer.cancel();
        }
    }
}
```

In addition to this method, the specification has removed the restrictions that required the use of `javax.ejb.Timer` and `javax.ejb.TimerHandlereferences` only inside a bean.

Harmonizing with JMS's novelties

A **Message-Driven Bean** (**MDB**) is a kind of a JMS Message listener allowing Java EE applications to process messages asynchronously. To define such a bean, simply decorate a simple POJO class with @MessageDriven annotation and make it implement the javax.jms.MessageListener interface. This interface makes available to the MDB the onMessage method that will be called each time a new message is posted in the queue associated with the bean. That's why you have to put inside this method the business logic for the processing of incoming messages. The following code gives an example of an MDB that notifies you when a new message arrives by writing in the console:

```
@MessageDriven(activationConfig = {
    @ActivationConfigProperty(propertyName = "destinationType",
                              propertyValue = "javax.jms.Queue"),
    @ActivationConfigProperty(propertyName = "destinationLookup",
                              propertyValue = "jms/messageQueue")
})
public class MessageBeanExample implements MessageListener {

    public MessageBeanExample() {
    }

    @Override
    public void onMessage(Message message) {
        try{
          System.out.println("You have received a new message of type
          : "+message.getJMSType());
        }catch(Exception ex){
            ex.printStackTrace();
        }
    }
}
```

Given the changes in JMS 2.0 Specification, the EJB 3.2 Specification has a revised list of JMS MDB activation properties to conform to the list of standard properties. These properties are: destinationLookup, connectionFactoryLookup, clientId, subscriptionName, and shareSubscriptions. In addition, it has added the ability in MDB to implement a no-method message listener, resulting in the exposure of all public methods of the bean as message listener methods.

Other improvements

As we said earlier, the EJB 3.1 Specification has given developers the opportunity to test EJB applications outside a full Java EE server. This was made possible through an embeddable `EJBContainer`. The following example demonstrates how to test an EJB using an embeddable `EJBContainer`:

```
@Test
public void testAddition(){
    Map<String, Object> properties = new HashMap<String, Object>();
    properties.put(EJBContainer.APP_NAME,
"chapter05EmbeddableEJBContainer");
    properties.put(EJBContainer.MODULES, new File("target\\classes"));
    EJBContainer container = javax.ejb.embeddable.EJBContainer.
createEJBContainer(properties);
    try {
        NewSessionBean bean = (NewSessionBean) container.getContext().
lookup("java:global/chapter05EmbeddableEJBContainer/NewSessionBean");
        int restult = bean.addition(10, 10);
        Assert.assertEquals(20, restult);
    } catch (NamingException ex) {
        Logger.getLogger(AppTest.class.getName()).log(Level.FINEST,
null, ex);
    } finally {
        container.close();
    }
}
```

Since the embeddable `EJBContainer` reference by maven was not up-to-date while writing this book (which caused the error "No EJBContainer provider available"), I directly addressed the `glassfish-embedded-static-shell.jar` file in the following way:

- Maven variable declaration:

```
<properties>
    <glassfish.installed.embedded.container>glassfish_dir\lib\
embedded\glassfish-embedded-static-shell.jar</glassfish.installed.
embedded.container>
</properties>
```

- Declaration of dependence:

```
<dependency>
    <groupId>glassfish-embedded-static-shell</groupId>
    <artifactId>glassfish-embedded-static-shell</artifactId>
    <version>3.2</version>
    <scope>system</scope>
    <systemPath>${glassfish.installed.embedded.container}</
systemPath>
</dependency>
```

During operation, the embeddable `EJBContainer` acquires resources that would
normally be released at the end of the process to allow other applications to take
advantage of the maximum power of the machine. In the previous version of the
specification, a developer used the `EJBContainer.close()` method in a `finally`
block to perform this task. But, with the `try-with-resources` statement introduced
in Java SE 7, EJB 3.2 added the implementation of the `java.lang.AutoCloseable`
interface in the `EJBContainer` class to free the developer from a task that could
easily be forgotten and have negative repercussions on the performance of a
machine. Now, the embeddable `EJBContainer` will be automatically closed at
the end of a statement, provided that it is declared as a resource in a `try-with-resources`
`resources` statement. Thus, we no longer need a `finally` block like in the earlier
example, which simplifies the code. The following example demonstrates how to
take advantage of the `try-with-resources` statement while testing EJB with an
embeddable `EJBContainer`:

```
@Test
public void testAddition(){
    //...
    try(EJBContainer container = javax.ejb.embeddable.EJBContainer.cre
ateEJBContainer(properties);) {
        //...
    } catch (NamingException ex) {
        Logger.getLogger(AppTest.class.getName()).log(Level.FINEST,
null, ex);
    }
}
```

The final improvement of this specification concerns removal of the restriction on
obtaining the current class loader when you want to access files or directories in the
file system from a bean.

Putting it all together

The example that will allow us to put together most of the APIs already studied since the first chapter, is an online preregistration site. In this example, we will not write any code. We limit ourselves to the presentation of an analysis of a problem that will help you understand how to use each of the pieces of code that are used to illustrate points in this book, in order to make a quality application based on the latest functionality of Java EE 7.

Presenting the project

The virtual enterprise software technology has received from a private university the order for creating an application to manage the preregistration of students online (candidate registration, validation of applications, and notifications of different candidates) and provide a real-time chat room for connected students. Furthermore, for statistical purposes, the system will allow the ministry of education access to certain information from a heterogeneous application.

The system called ONPRINS must be robust, efficient, and available 24 x 7 during periods of registration.

The business domain model in the following diagram represents the main objects of our system (the required application will be built based on these objects):

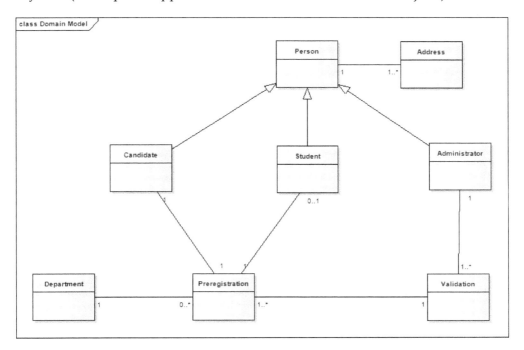

Disclaimer

These diagrams have been designed and built in Enterprise Architect, by Sparx Systems.

Use Case Diagram (UCD)

The following diagram represents all the features that will be supported by our system. We have three actors as follows:

- A Candidate is any user wishing to preregister for a department. To this end, it has the ability to view the list of departments, select a department, and complete and submit the application form. Through a chat room, he/she can share his/her ideas with all candidates connected with respect to a given theme.

- An Administrator is a special user who has the right to run the validation process of preregistration. It is this process that creates the students and sends e-mails to different candidates to let them know whether they have been selected or not.

- The Ministry of Education is a secondary actor of the system; it seeks access to the number of preregistered students and the list of students during an academic year.

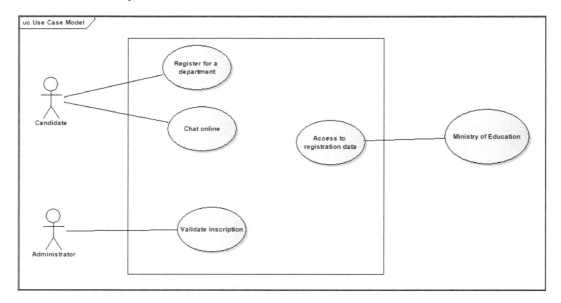

Class diagram

The following class diagram shows all the main classes used for the realization of our online preregistration. This diagram also highlights the relationships that exist between different classes.

The CandidateSessionBean class is a bean that records the preregistration of candidates through registerCandidate method. It also provides methods for accessing all the registered candidates (listOfCandidates) and preregistered students (listOfStudents).

The InscriptionValidationBean class contains the startValidationBatchJob method which, as its name suggests, launches batch processing to validate the preregistration and notify different candidates. Batch processing presented here is the chunk type in which the ValidationReader class is used to read the data useful for validation, the ValidationProcessor class is used to validate the preregistration, and the ValidationWriter class is used to notify the candidate. This class also serves to create a student when the candidate is selected. As you can see, in order to send an e-mail, the ValidationWriter class firstly sends a JMS message through MsgSenderSessionBean to the component responsible for sending the e-mail. This allows us to avoid blockages in ValidationWriter when there is a connection breakdown. Also, in the batch process, we have the listener ValidationJobListener, which enables us to record a certain amount of information in the validation table at the end of batch processing.

For the sake of simplicity and reusability, navigation between web pages during the preregistration of a candidate (departmentList.xhtml, acceptanceConditions.xhtml, identificationInformation.xhtml, contactInformation.xhtml, medicalInformation.xhtml, schoolInformation.xhtml, and InformationValidation.xhtml) will be made using the Faces Flow. On the other hand, the content of various pages will be structured with the Resource Library Contracts and communication in the chat room will be managed using WebSocket; it is for this reason that you have the ChatServerEndPoint class, which is the server endpoint for this communication.

The execution of the validation process of preregistration is made from the inscriptionValidation.xhtml facelet. In order to give the administrator a feedback on the progress of the validation process, the facelet will contain a progress bar updated in real time, which leads us once again to use the WebSocket protocol.

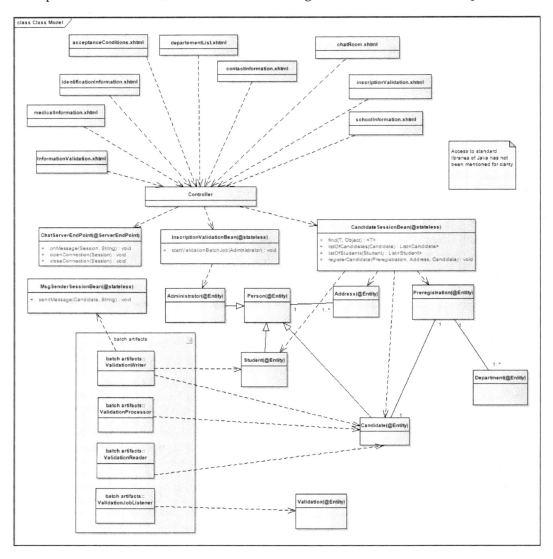

Component diagram

The following diagram shows the various components that constitute our system. As you can see, the exchange of data between the application of the ministry and ONPRINS will be through web services, which aims to make both systems completely independent from one another, while our system uses a connector to have access to user information stored on the ERP system of the university.

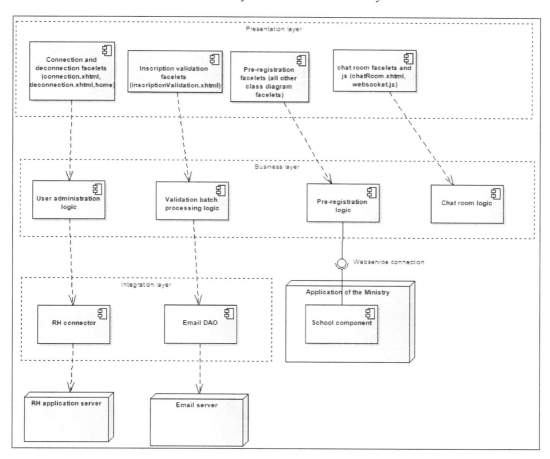

Summary

As promised, in this chapter we presented the innovations introduced by EJBs, and then focused on the analysis and design of an application for online preregistration. In this exercise, we were able to look at practical cases allowing us to use almost all of the concepts already discussed (WebSocket and Faces Flow) and discover new concepts (web service, connector, and Java e-mail). In the next chapter, we will focus on these new concepts in order to try to answer the following question: when and how should we implement these concepts?

6
Communicating with External Systems

In this chapter, we are going to add the possibility to communicate with different systems in our application. Technically, we will resolve a systems integration problem. System integration problems include several cases: two applications that exchange data synchronously or asynchronously, an application that accesses information provided by another, an application that executes processes implemented in another, and so on. Given the number of solutions that exist today, it is necessary to know which one to choose depending on the problem, hence the importance of this chapter. At the end of this chapter, you will be able to choose an integration solution and have an overview of the changes made in the following APIs:

- JavaMail
- Java EE connector architecture
- Java message service
- JAX-RS: Java API for RESTful Web Services

JavaMail

The JavaMail 1.5 Specification was developed under JSR 919. This section just gives you an overview of improvements in the API. The complete document specification (for more information) can be downloaded from `http://jcp.org/aboutJava/communityprocess/mrel/jsr919/index2.html`.

Sending e-mails in Java

The expansion of the Internet has greatly facilitated communication across the world through electronic messages (e-mail). Today, people at the ends of the earth can exchange information in a very short time. In order for this to be done, there must be a mail server for storage of data exchanged and clients (for example, Outlook) for sending and retrieving data. Communication between these elements requires different types of protocols, for example, **SMTP (Simple Mail Transport Protocol)** for sending mails, **POP3 (Post Office Protocol)** for receiving mails, **IMAP (Internet Message Access Protocol)** for receiving e-mails. This multitude of protocols can pose a problem to the developer.

Given the multitude of protocols and the difficulties of low-level programming, the Java language provides the **JavaMail** API in order to simplify sending and retrieving e-mails regardless of the underlying protocols. But the JavaMail API is not enough; because it was designed to handle the transmission aspect of the message (connection parameter, source, destination, subject, and so on), the body of the message is managed by **JavaBeans Activation Framework (JAF framework)**. That is why, in addition to the `mail.jar` library, you have to import the `activation.jar` library.

Sending an e-mail via the SMTP protocol

Sending an e-mail using JavaMail is done as follows:

1. Obtain the `session` object. This object encapsulates various information such as the address of the mail server. The following code shows how to get an object of type `Session`:

```
Properties prop = System.getProperties();
//serveurAddress is the host of you mail server
prop.put("mail.smtp.host", serveurAddress);
Session session = Session.getDefaultInstance(prop,null);
```

2. Construct the message. To send an e-mail, it is necessary to define some parameters such as the content of the e-mail, the sender, and destination. In addition to these settings, you may need to specify the subject of your e-mail and its header. All this is made possible through the `MimeMessage` class that offers several methods to construct a message for a given session. The following code shows how to get an object of type `MimeMessage` and build a mail to send:

```
Message msg = new MimeMessage(session);
msg.setFrom(new InternetAddress
  ("xxx-university@yahoo.fr"));
InternetAddress[] internetAddresses = new InternetAddress[1];
internetAddresses[0] = new InternetAddress("malindaped@yahoo.fr");
```

```
msg.setRecipients(
  Message.RecipientType.TO,internetAddresses);
msg.setSubject("Pre-inscription results");
msg.setText("Dear Malinda, we inform you that …");
```

3. Send the message. We send a message in one line with the `Transport` class. The following code shows how to send the message:

    ```
    Transport.send(msg);
    ```

The following code shows how to send the results of preregistration for individual candidates from a Gmail account. As you can see, the Gmail sender account and its password are passed as a parameter to the `send` method. This allows the application to be authenticated by the server when sending the message. To test the sending code associated with this chapter, you need to have a Gmail account and replace `username` with the username of your account and `user_password` with the password of this account.

The following code is an example of sending an e-mail via Gmail SMTP server by using JavaMail API:

```java
public class MailSender {

  private final String userName = "username@gmail.com";
  private final String userPassword = "user_password";
  private Session session;

  public MailSender() {
    Properties props = new Properties();
    props.put("mail.smtp.auth", "true");
    props.put("mail.smtp.starttls.enable", "true");
    props.put("mail.smtp.host", "smtp.gmail.com");
    props.put("mail.smtp.port", "587");

    session = Session.getInstance(props, null);
  }

  public void sendMesage(String message, String toAddress) {
    try {

      Message msg = new MimeMessage(session);
      InternetAddress[] internetAddresses =
        new InternetAddress[1];
      internetAddresses[0] = new InternetAddress(toAddress);
      msg.setRecipients
        (Message.RecipientType.TO, internetAddresses);
      msg.setSubject("Pre-inscription results");
```

```
      msg.setText(message);

      Transport.send(msg, userName, userPassword);
    } catch (Exception ex) {
      ex.printStackTrace();
    }


  }
}
```

Of course, the JavaMail API provides the ability to retrieve messages, attach documents to your messages, write messages in HTML format, and do lots of other things.

The latest improvements in action

Although it is affected by a maintenance release, the JavaMail 1.5 Specification has undergone many changes. The most important can be grouped into three categories, which are: addition of annotations, addition of methods, and changing of some access modifiers.

The added annotations

In all, JavaMail 1.5 introduced two new annotations (`@MailSessionDefinition` and `@MailSessionDefinitions`) to configure JavaMail session resources in a Java EE 7 application server.

The `@MailSessionDefinition` annotation contains several parameters (see the `Java` class in the following code) with the goal of offering the possibility to define a Mail Session that will be registered in any valid Java EE namespace and accessed by other components through the **JNDI**.

The following code highlights the attributes of `@MailSessionDefinition` annotation:

```
public @interface MailSessionDefinition {

  String description() default "";

  String name();

  String storeProtocol() default "";

  String transportProtocol() default "";

  String host() default "";
```

```
    String user() default "";

    String password() default "";

    String from() default "";

    String[] properties() default {};
}
```

With this annotation, we can now define and use objects of Session type as
in the case of the following code which is an example to show how to use
@MailSessionDefinition:

```
@MailSessionDefinition(
  name = "java:app/env/MyMailSession",
  transportProtocol = "SMTP",
  user = "username@gmail.com",
  password = "user_password"
  //...
)
@WebServlet(name = "MailSenderServlet")
public class MailSenderServlet extends HttpServlet {

  @Resource(lookup="java:app/env/MyMailSession")
  Session session;

  public void doPost(HttpServletRequest request, HttpServletResponse
response)
  throws IOException, ServletException {

    //...
  }
}
```

While the @MailSessionDefinition annotation allows us to define MailSession,
@MailSessionDefinitions annotation allows us to configure many
MailSession instances. The following code shows how to define two
MailSession using instances @MailSessionDefinitions at a time:

```
@MailSessionDefinitions(
        { @MailSessionDefinition(name = "java:/en/..."),
        @MailSessionDefinition(name = "java:/en/...") }
)
```

The added methods

In order to ease the developer's work, JavaMail 1.5 added new methods that provide really interesting shortcuts. For example, the addition of the `Transport.send(msg, username, password)` method avoids creating additional objects for authentication parameters when sending the message. Before this, authentication parameters were defined at the `session` object and as you can see with the following code:

```
Session session = Session.getInstance(props,
  new javax.mail.Authenticator() {
  protected PasswordAuthentication getPasswordAuthentication() {
    return new PasswordAuthentication(username, password);
  }
});
```

As another example of an added method, you have the `Message.getSession()` method, which allows you to access the `session` type object that was used to create the message. This may prevent you from having to drag the session throughout your treatment. The last added method that we will talk about is the `MimeMessage.reply(replyToAll, setAnswered)` method, which, due to the second parameter, allows you to automatically add a `Re` prefix to the subject line when you respond, for example, to a message.

The changing of some access modifiers

Concerning access modifiers, the JavaMail 1.5 Specification has put an emphasis on good practice in some classes and facilitated the extension of others.

You will see, for example, that the access modifiers of the protected fields in the final classes of the `javax.mail.search` package have been changed to private. In fact, it is not important that the final class contains protected fields with public `getter/setter` method. So it is better to make them private and let `getter/setter` be public so that we can access/edit their values from outside.

Still, in the changing of access modifier, JavaMail 1.5 has transformed the fields `cachedContent` (of classes `MimeBodyPart` and `MimeMessage`) and `MimeMultipart` class's fields from private to protected in order to facilitate the extension of the relevant classes.

Java EE Connector Architecture (JCA)

The Java EE Connector Architecture 1.7 Specification was developed under JSR 322. This section just gives you an overview of improvements in the API. The complete document specification (for more information) can be downloaded from `http://jcp.org/aboutJava/communityprocess/final/jsr322/index.html`.

What is JCA?

Generally, **Enterprise Information Systems** (EISs) of large companies are composed of a number of tools such as **Enterprise Resource Planning** applications (**ERP**, that is **SAP**), **Customer Relationship Management** applications (**CRM**, that is `salesforce.com`), mainframe Transaction Processing applications, legacy applications and Database Systems (such as Oracle). In such an environment, the development of a new solution may require access to one or more of these tools to retrieve information or perform processing: we then talk of an **Enterprise Application Integration** (**EAI**). In the absence of a standard solution, this integration will be costly to both vendors and developers. Vendors will develop APIs to manage communication between different kinds of servers and developers will address EISs case by case and will implement the technical features (connection polling, transaction security mechanism, and so on) required by the application. Hence the need for JCA.

The Java EE Connector Architecture (JCA) is a specification that aims to standardize access to heterogeneous existing EISs from Java EE platforms. To this end, it defines a set of contracts that enable developers to access the different EISs seamlessly from a common interface called the **Common Client Interface** (CCI). For those who have already been working with **JDBC**, understanding of the functioning of JCA is a little easier. A JCA connector consists of two main elements:

- **Common Client Interface** (CCI): This API is to EISs as JDBC is to databases. In other words, the CCI defines a standard client API that allows components to access EISs and perform processing.

- **Resource Adapter**: This is a specific implementation of the CCI for a given EIS. It is provided by the vendor, which guarantees the execution of the features of its EIS through the JCA. The Resource Adapter, is packaged in a `.rar` archive called `Resource Adapter Module`, and it must obey some contracts (system level contracts) in order to be integrated into a Java EE platform and take advantage of services such as Connection, Transaction, and Security Management.

That said, you can consider using JCA when you want to access an EIS that offers a Resource Adapter.

JCA in action

Failing to take a concrete example that shows you how to access the list of employees managed by SAP with a connector (which would be very long), to allow you to understand the essential features), the following code shows you just an overview of the use of the JCA API. These include the general principle of the connection, the possibility of data manipulation, and disconnection.

For those who wish to go further, GlassFish offers a complete example of implementing a connector to access a mail server, and the tutorial available at http://www.ibm.com/developerworks/java/tutorials/j-jca/index.html, provides you additional information.

The following code is a overview of interactions with a resource adapter:

```
try {
  javax.naming.Context ic = new InitialContext();
  javax.resource.cci.ConnectionFactory cf =
  (ConnectionFactory)
  ic.lookup("java:comp/env/eis/ConnectionFactory");
  //Connection
  javax.resource.cci.Connection ctx = cf.getConnection();

  System.out.println(
    "Information about the result set functionality "
    + "supported by the connected EIS : " +
    ctx.getResultSetInfo());

  System.out.println
    ("Metadata about the connection : " + ctx.getMetaData());

  //Get object for accessing EIS functions
  javax.resource.cci.Interaction interaction =
    ctx.createInteraction();

  //Get record factory
  javax.resource.cci.RecordFactory rfact = cf.getRecordFactory();

  javax.resource.cci.IndexedRecord input =
    rfact.createIndexedRecord("<recordName>");
  javax.resource.cci.IndexedRecord output =
    rfact.createIndexedRecord("<recordName>");
  //Look up a preconfigured InteractionSpec
  javax.resource.cci.InteractionSpec interSp = ... ;
  interaction.execute(interSp, input, output);
```

```
    int index_of_element = ...;//index of element to return
    System.out.println
      ("The result : "+output.get(index_of_element));
    //close
    interaction.close();
    ctx.close();
  } catch (Exception ex) {
    ex.printStackTrace();
  }
```

Latest improvements

Talking about novelty, the Java EE Connector Architecture 1.7 was slightly improved. Indeed, in this specification, it is more a matter of clarification and requirements statements. That said, JCA 1.7 has introduced the following changes:

- It insists on the availability of the the application component environment namespace of the endpoint to the resource adapter when the `endpointActivation` and `endpointDeactivation` methods are called

- It adds `ConnectionFactoryDefinition` and `AdministeredObjectDefinition` annotations for defining and configuring the resource adapter's resources

- It clarifies the behavior of the dependency injection when Managed JavaBeans are used as CDI-managed Beans

Java Message Service (JMS)

The Java Message Service 2.0 Specification was developed under JSR 343. This section just gives you an overview of improvements in the API. The complete document specification (for more information) can be downloaded from `http://jcp.org/aboutJava/communityprocess/final/jsr343/index.html`.

When to use JMS

JMS is a Java API for interacting with **Message Oriented Middleware (MOM)**. This type of middleware is born from the need to solve observed limits in synchronous connections. This is because synchronous connections are susceptible to network failures and require that the connected systems are available at the same time. Hence, the MOMs offer an integration system based on the exchange of messages that can be treated synchronously or asynchronously depending on the availability of the integrated systems.

The following image shows an architecture in which systems communicate through MOM:

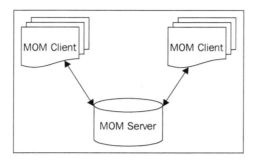

Based on the foregoing, we conclude that JMS can be used in the following cases:

- Transaction processing large amount of data (for example, synchronization of databases) through an unstable network
- Communication between systems that are not always available simultaneously
- Sending of data to multiple systems
- Asynchronous processing

To finish with this point, you should notice that the establishment of an integration system based on JMS requires that all components that need to be integrated be under your control. Hence, JMS would be better for the integration of internal solutions of a company.

The latest improvements in action

Released in March 2002, the JMS 1.1 Specification was getting old and heavy compared to other APIs of the Java EE platform that have been simplified through the evolution of the platform. Based on this observation, you will understand why one of the main goals of JMS 2.0 API was to update the API so that it can be as simple as the other APIs of the platform and can integrate easily with them. To make this possible, several areas have been reviewed; these include the reduction of **boilerplate** code, removing redundant items, adding new features, and integration of the novelties of the Java language.

New features

In the JMS 2.0 Specification, three new features are highlighted: sending of messages asynchronously, delivery delay, and modification of the JMSXDeliveryCount message property.

Sending messages asynchronously

In synchronous processing, if a method A invokes a method B, method A will remain blocked until the method B has completed. This can induce a waste of time. To overcome this problem, JMS 2.0 provides a set of methods to send messages asynchronously without losing sight of the progress of the operation. The following code demonstrates how to send messages asynchronously. The method `setAsync()` takes a listener as a parameter, which allows you to be informed at the end of the process or when an exception is thrown. If the listener is not null, the message will be sent asynchronously (the process will be performed by another thread different from the caller's thread). Otherwise, the message will be sent synchronously.

```
public void sendMessageAsynchronously
  (ConnectionFactory cfactory,Queue destination){
  try(JMSContext context = cfactory.createContext();){
    context.createProducer().setAsync
      (new Completion()).send(destination, "Hello world");
  }
}


class Completion implements CompletionListener{

  public void onCompletion(Message message) {
    System.out.println("message sent successfully");
  }

  public void onException(Message message, Exception ex) {
    System.out.println(ex.getMessage());
  }
}
```

Delivery delay

In addition to the possibility of sending messages asynchronously, JMS now permits us to defer the time of delivery of a message already in the **broker**, which is a MOM server. After sending, the message will be stored at the broker, but it will stay unknown to the receiver until the time fixed by the sender. The message of the following code will be delivered to the recipient at least one hour after sending.

```
public void sendMessageWithDelay(ConnectionFactory cfactory,Queue
destination){
  try(JMSContext context = cfactory.createContext();){
    context.createProducer().setDeliveryDelay(1000*60*60).
send(destination, "Hello world");
  }
}
```

Handling of the JMSXDeliveryCount message property

Since Version 1.1, the JMS Specification has defined an optional JMSXDeliveryCount message property, which can be used to determine the messages that were delivered more than once and apply an action when the number of deliveries exceeds the maximum value. But, because the management of this property was optional, all providers had no obligation to increment it, which had the effect of making applications that used it non portable. The JMS 2.0 Specification has introduced this as standard, to allow us to customize the management of **poisonous messages** in a portable way. A poisonous message is a JMS message that has exceeded the maximum number of deliveries for a given receiver. The following code shows how to retrieve the JMSXDeliveryCount message property and specify the action to be taken when one message has been delivered more that five time:

```
public class JmsMessageListener implements MessageListener {

    @Override
    public void onMessage(Message message) {
      try {
        int jmsxDeliveryCount =
          message.getIntProperty("JMSXDeliveryCount");
        //...
        if(jmsxDeliveryCount > 5){
          // do something
        }
      } catch (JMSException ex) {
        ex.printStackTrace();
      }
    }
}
```

Simplification of the API

The JMS 2.0 Specification introduces three new interfaces (JMSContext, JMSProducer, and JMSConsumer) which contribute to the elimination of boilerplate code and simplifying the API. It is important to note that these interfaces (which constitute the simplified API) co-exist with the old interfaces to provide an alternative. So JMSContext replaces the Connection and Session objects, JMSProducer replaces the MessageProducer object, and JMSConsumer replaces the MessageConsumer object in the old version. As you can see in the following code, the difference between the two approaches is very clear. In the sending method based on JMS API 1.1 (sendMessageJMSWithOldAPI), we note: an excessive object creation, a mandatory throw of an exception, and a need to explicitly close connections.

Whereas, in the sending method based on JMS API 2.0 (sendMessageJMSWithNewdAPI), we have: the try-with-resources statement that saves the developer from having to explicitly close the connection and a send code reduced to the essentials that would fit on one line if we had injected JMSContext object.

```java
//Sending message with JMS 1.1
public void sendMessageJMSWithOldAPI(ConnectionFactory
connectionFactory, Queue destination) throws JMSException {
 Connection connection = connectionFactory.createConnection();
 try {
     Session session = connection.createSession(false, Session.AUTO_
ACKNOWLEDGE);
     MessageProducer messageProducer = session.
createProducer(destination);
     TextMessage textMessage = session.createTextMessage("Message send
with the old API");
     messageProducer.send(textMessage);
  } finally {
    connection.close();
  }
}

//Sending message with JMS 2.0
public void sendMessageJMSWithNewdAPI(ConnectionFactory
connectionFactory, Queue destination) {
     try (JMSContext context = connectionFactory.createContext();) {
         context.createProducer().send(destination, "Message send with
the new API");
     }
}
```

Java API for RESTful Web Services

The Java API for RESTful Web Services 2.0 Specification was developed under JSR 339. This section just gives you an overview of improvements in the API. The complete document specification (for more information) can be downloaded from http://jcp.org/aboutJava/communityprocess/final/jsr339/index.html.

When to use Web Services

A Web Service is a software system based on open standards (such as HTTP, XML, and URI) and designed to allow exchanges between applications across the network. By using these open standards, it has everything required to be the most suitable solution for integrating heterogeneous systems. However, as we saw when we were talking about JMS, the choice of an integration solution should be made after a series of questions: Is the network connection good? Are the processes transactional? Is the amount of data to be processed huge? Must processing be synchronous? and so on.

If after investigation, your choice is Web Services, you must now select the type of web service to implement : the **SOAP** Web Services based on SOAP (**Simple Object Access Protocol**) and XML, or RESTful Web Services that are focused on resource sharing and thus their functioning is modeled on the Web. In this book, we will only discuss RESTful Web Services.

JAX-RS in action

RESTful Web Services are a variant of Web Services in which any concepts that can be addressed (functionality or data) are considered as resources and therefore can be accessed through **Uniform Resource Identifiers** (**URIs**). Once located, the representation or state of the resource is transferred in the form of an XML or a JSON document. In the case of our online preregistration application, the resources may be the list of selected students and the representation will be in a JSON document.

JAX-RS is the Java API to implement RESTful Web Services. The following code demonstrates how to write a REST service that returns a list of all students who were selected:

```
@Path("students")
@Stateless
@Produces({MediaType.APPLICATION_JSON})
public class StudentInformation {

  @PersistenceContext(unitName = "integrationPU")
  private EntityManager em;

  @GET
  @Path("getListOfStudents")
  public List<Student> getListOfStudents(){
    TypedQuery<Student> query = em.createQuery
      ("SELECT s FROM Student s", Student.class);
    return query.getResultList();
  }
} }
```

The latest improvements in action

JAX-RS 2.0 not only simplified the implementation of RESTful Web Services, but also introduced new features in the API, among which we have client API, asynchronous processing, filters, and interceptors.

The Client API

Since Version 1.0, the JAX-RS Specification did not define client APIs to interact with a RESTful service. So, each implementation provided a proprietary API, which had the effect of limiting the portability of applications. JAX-RS 2.0 fills this gap by providing a standard client API.

The following code demonstrates the implementation of a client that will access the list of selected students through the REST service exposed in the preceding code:

```
String baseURI =
  "http://localhost:8080/chapter06EISintegration-web";
Client client = ClientBuilder.newClient();
WebTarget target = client.target
  (baseURI+"/rs-resources/students/getListOfStudents");
GenericType<List<Student>> list = new GenericType<List<Student>>() {};
List<Student> students =
  target.request(MediaType.APPLICATION_JSON).get(list);
```

Asynchronous processing

In addition to the standardization of the client API, JAX-RS 2.0 has integrated a feature already present in many of the APIs of the Java EE platform, which is asynchronous processing. It is now possible for a JAX-RS client to send requests or process responses asynchronously.

The following code demonstrates how a JAX-RS client can perform a get request asynchronously and wait for the response passively. As shown in the code, the execution of a JAX-RS request asynchronously requires a call to the `async()` method. This method returns an object of type `AsyncInvoker` whose get, post, delete, and put methods allow us to obtain the object type `Future` that will be used for further processing of the response.

The following code is an example of the execution of a asynchronous process in a JAX-RS client:

```
public class AppAsynchronousRestfulClient {

  public static void main(String[] args) {
    String baseURI =
      "http://localhost:8080/chapter06EISintegration-web";
```

```
String location = "/rs-resources";
String method = "/students/getListOfAllStudentsAs";
Client client = ClientBuilder.newClient();
WebTarget target =
  (WebTarget) client.target(baseURI+location+method);
System.out.println("Before response : "+new Date());
Future<String> response = target.request
  (MediaType.APPLICATION_JSON).async().get(String.class);

new PassiveWaiting(response).start();

System.out.println("After PassiveWaiting : "+new Date());
}

static class PassiveWaiting extends Thread {
  Future<String> response;

  public PassiveWaiting(Future<String> response){
    this.response = response;
  }

  public void run(){
    try{
      System.out.println("response :
        "+response.get()+", time : "+new Date());
    }catch(Exception ex){
      ex.printStackTrace();
    }
  }
}
}
```

To ensure that the processing is executed asynchronously, we have defined a break of 20 seconds in the getListOfAllStudentsAs method before executing the JPQL queries. The following code,which is a simulation of a slow processing, shows the contents of the method executed by the client:

```
@GET
@Path("getListOfAllStudentsAs")
public List<Student> getListOfAllStudentsAs() {
  try{
    Thread.sleep(20*1000);//20 seconds
  }catch(Exception ex){}
  TypedQuery<Student> query = em.createQuery
    ("SELECT s FROM Student s", Student.class);
  return query.getResultList();
}
```

Similarly, the JAX-RS servers are able to run processes asynchronously. The method that contains the instructions to perform the task asynchronously must inject an object of type `AsyncResponse` as a method parameter with the `@Suspended` annotation. However, you should know that the asynchronous mode of the server differs from the asynchronous mode of the client; the former consists of suspending the client connection from which the request was send during the processing of the request before resuming it later through the `resume()` method of the object `AsyncResponse`. The method itself will not run asynchronously. To make it asynchronous, you must either delegate the process to a thread (that is what we did in the `getListOfAllStudentsAs2` method of the following example), or decorate it with the `@Asynchronous` annotation. The following code demonstrates how to perform asynchronous processing at the server side.

The following code is an example of the execution of a process asynchronously in a JAX-RS server:

```
@Path("students")
@Stateless
@Produces({MediaType.APPLICATION_JSON, MediaType.APPLICATION_XML})
public class StudentInformation {

  @PersistenceContext(unitName = "integrationPU")
  private EntityManager em;

  @Resource(lookup =
    "java:comp/DefaultManagedScheduledExecutorService")
  ManagedExecutorService taskExecutor;

  @GET
  @Path("getListOfAllStudentsAs2")
  public void getListOfAllStudentsAs2
    (final @Suspended AsyncResponse response) {
      System.out.println("before time : "+new Date());
      taskExecutor.submit(
      new Runnable() {
        public void run() {
          String queryString = "SELECT s FROM Student s
            WHERE 1 = 1";
          TypedQuery<Student> query = em.createQuery
            (queryString, Student.class);

          List<Student> studentList = query.getResultList();
          try {
            Thread.sleep(10 * 1000);//1 second
          } catch (Exception ex) {
```

```
            }
            response.resume(studentList);
        }
    });
    System.out.println("After time : "+new Date());
    }
}
```

Filters and entity interceptors

Another big ticket of the JAX-RS 2.0 Specification is the introduction of two mechanisms for interception: filters and interceptors. These new features bring to the specification a standard way to intercept processing in order to seamlessly manage security, compression, encoding, logging, editing, and auditing of exchanges between a JAX-RS server and the different clients that will access the server resources.

Although the two concepts are very similar (as they all relate to interception), we must say that the filter is often used for the processing of the headers of requests or responses. Whereas, interceptors are generally set up to manipulate the content of messages.

Filters

The JAX-RS 2.0 specification defines four types of filters: two types of filters on each side (client and server). On the client side, one filter that must be run before sending the HTTP request implements the `ClientRequestFilter` interface and the other filter, which must be run immediately after the receipt of the response from the server, (but before the control is rendered to the application) implements the `ClientResponseFilter` interface. On the server side, the filter that will be executed before the access to a JAX-RS resource implements the `ContainerRequestFilter` interface and the filter that will run just before the response is sent to the client implements the `ContainerResponseFilter` interface. The following code shows an example of `ContainerRequestFilter` implementation that verifies the information that ensures a secure access to the resources available to external users of our online preregistration application. The `@Provider` annotation on top of the `MyJaxRsRequestFilter` class in the following code allows the filter to be automatically discovered by the container and applied to all resources of the server. Failing to use this annotation, you must manually registered the filter.

The following code is an example of `ContainerRequestFilter` implementation:

```
@Provider
public class MyJaxRsRequestFilter implements ContainerRequestFilter {

  @Override
  public void filter(ContainerRequestContext crq) {
    //       If the user has not been authenticated
    if(crq.getSecurityContext().getUserPrincipal() == null)
      throw new WebApplicationException(Status.UNAUTHORIZED);

    List<MediaType> supportedMedia =
      crq.getAcceptableMediaTypes();
    if("GET".equals(crq.getMethod()) &&
      !supportedMedia.contains(MediaType.APPLICATION_JSON_TYPE))
      throw new WebApplicationException
        (Status.UNSUPPORTED_MEDIA_TYPE);

    //       external users must only access student methods
    String path = crq.getUriInfo().getPath();
    if(!path.startsWith("/students"))
      throw new WebApplicationException(Status.FORBIDDEN);

    List<String> encoding = crq.getHeaders().get
      ("accept-encoding");
    //   If the client does not support the gzip compression
    if(!encoding.toString().contains("gzip"))
      throw new WebApplicationException
        (Status.EXPECTATION_FAILED);
  }
}
```

Entity interceptors

In addition to the differences noted between filters and entity interceptors, JAX-RS provides two types of entity interceptors instead of four. There is a reader interceptor that implements the `ReaderInterceptor` interface and a writer interceptor, which implements the `WriterInterceptor` interface. Due to the elements that they are supposed to handle (message bodies), interceptors can be used to compress large content to optimize network utilization; they can also be used for some processing such as the generation and verification of digital signatures.

Given that the database of our online preregistration application will contain thousands of students, the following code demonstrates how we can take advantage of interceptors in the data exchange with the Ministry of Education in order to avoid network overloading when transmitting information about students.

The following code shows the implementation of WriterInterceptor (on the server side) that will compress data to send to the JAX-RS client. The @ZipResult annotation allows us to bind the interceptor only to some JAX-RS resources. If we remove this annotation, all JAX-RS resources of our application will be automatically compressed.

The following code is an example of a WriterInterceptor implemention:

```
@ZipResult
@Provider
public class MyGzipWriterJaxRsInterceptor implements
WriterInterceptor{

    @Override
    public void aroundWriteTo(WriterInterceptorContext wic) throws
IOException {
        try (GZIPOutputStream gzipStream = new GZIPOutputStream(wic.
getOutputStream());) {
            wic.setOutputStream(gzipStream);
            wic.proceed();
        }
    }
}
```

To bind the MyGzipWriterJaxRsInterceptor interceptor to a resource, we will only decorate the given resource with the @ZipResult annotation. The following code demonstrates how to bind MyGzipWriterJaxRsInterceptor interceptor to a resource so that its representation can be always compressed before being sent to the client.

The following code is an example of of interceptor binding:

```
@GET
@ZipResult
@Path("getListOfAllStudentsGzip")
public List<Student> getListOfAllStudentsGzip() {
  TypedQuery<Student> query = em.createQuery
    ("SELECT s FROM Student s", Student.class);
  return query.getResultList();
}
```

The following code is an example of the declaration of `@ZipResult` annotation:

```
@NameBinding
@Target({ ElementType.TYPE, ElementType.METHOD })
@Retention(value = RetentionPolicy.RUNTIME)
public @interface ZipResult {}
```

The following code shows the implementation of the `ReaderInterceptor` interface (on the client side) that will decompress the data compressed by the server with the `MyGzipWriterJaxRsInterceptor` class:.

```
public class MyGzipReaderJaxRsInterceptor implements ReaderInterceptor
{
    @Override
    public Object aroundReadFrom(ReaderInterceptorContext context)
throws IOException {
        try (InputStream inputStream = context.getInputStream();) {
            context.setInputStream(new GZIPInputStream(inputStream));
            return context.proceed();
        }
    }
}
```

To bind the interceptor to a particular client, we will use the `register` method of the `Client` object. The following code demonstrates how to associate an interceptor or a filter to a JAX-RS Client:

```
public static void main(String[] args) throws IOException {
  String baseURI = "http://localhost:8080/
    chapter06EISintegration-web";
  String location = "/rs-resources";
  String method = "/students/getListOfAllStudentsGzip";
  //client creation and registration of the interceptor/filter
  Client client = ClientBuilder.newClient()
    .register(MyGzipReaderJaxRsInterceptor.class);
  WebTarget target = (WebTarget)
    client.target(baseURI + location + method);
  System.out.println
    ("response : " + target.request(MediaType.APPLICATION_JSON)
    .get(String.class));
}
```

Summary

During the analysis of the online preregistration application presented in the previous chapter, we realized that our system should communicate with other systems. This chapter has given us the knowledge to identify and implement the best way to exchange data with different kinds of heterogeneous systems. In the next chapter, we will revisit some concepts that we have used in a natural way so that you have a better understanding of them.

7
Annotations and CDI

Right up to this moment, we had to use annotations and dependency injections without trying to understand how they work. This chapter therefore aims to present and highlight improvements in the relevant APIs. The APIs concerned are:

- Common annotations for the Java Platform 1.2
- Contexts and Dependency Injection 1.1

Common annotations for the Java platform

The common annotations for the Java platform 1.2 Specification was developed under JSR 250. This section just gives you an overview of improvements in the API. The complete document specification (for more information) can be downloaded from `http://jcp.org/aboutJava/communityprocess/mrel/jsr250/index.html`.

The goal of this specification

Annotations are a form of metadata that are generally used to describe, configure, or mark elements (such as class, method, and attribute) of Java code. In the following code, we use the `@Stateless` annotation to configure `MySessionBean` class as a stateless session bean, we use the `@Deprecated` annotation to mark `oldMethod()` method as obsolete, and finally we set the `save()` method with the `@TransactionAttribute` annotation so that it will always use a dedicated transaction.

```
@Stateless
public class MySessionBean {

  @Deprecated
  public void oldMethod(){}
```

```
    @TransactionAttribute(TransactionAttributeType.REQUIRES_NEW)
    public void save(){}
}
```

The annotations have been integrated into the Java language since JDK 5 and they are now widely used in many APIs. To avoid redefining some annotations in several APIs, the JCP developed the common annotations for the Java platform specification with the goal of regrouping annotations that are common to different Java EE APIs, which avoids redundancy and facilitates the maintenance of regrouped annotations. In the following code, we have the example of the @Resource annotation from the common annotations for the Java platform API , which permits us to access an object of type SessionContext in a web container and in an EJB container.

```
@Stateless
public class MySessionBean {

  @javax.annotation.Resource
  private SessionContext sctx;

  //...
}
@ManagedBean
public class MyJsfManagedBean {
  @javax.annotation.Resource
  private SessionContext sctx;
  //...
}
```

Building your own annotation

Although there are already several annotations, Java offers the opportunity to create new custom annotations if you need. To do this, you should know that an annotation is declared as a Java interface. The only difference is that, in the case of the annotation the keyword interface must be preceded by the character @. The following code shows the declaration of the custom annotation Unfinished. This annotation contains a parameter named message whose default value is Nothing has been done.

```
public @interface Unfinished {
  String message() default "Nothing has been done";
}
```

Once you declare your annotation, you must now define its characteristics. The basic characteristics of an annotation are defined through dedicated annotations contained in the java.lang.annotation package. These annotations are as follows:

- @Target: This is used to define the element types that can be annotated (such as class, method, and attribute), for example @Target({ElementType. METHOD, ElementType.TYPE})

- @Retention: This is used to define the retention level (such as RUNTIME, CLASS, or SOURCE) of your annotation, for example @Retention(RetentionPolicy. RUNTIME)

- @Inherited: This is used to say that the annotation will be automatically applied to classes that inherit from the class that has the annotation

- @Documented: This is used to make your annotation appear in the **Javadoc** of the code that contains it

It is important to note that there are other characteristics such as the scope (set using the @ScopeType) in the case of custom CDI scope annotations.

After all changes, our annotation takes the form shown in the following code. According to the settings, this annotation can decorate methods, types of objects (such as class, interface, or enum) and attributes. It will be removed at the compile time (because the retention level is SOURCE).

```
@Target({ElementType.METHOD, ElementType.TYPE, ElementType.FIELD})
@Retention(RetentionPolicy.SOURCE)
public @interface Unfinished {
  String message() default "Nothing has been done";
}
```

The following code demonstrates the usage of the Unfinished annotation:

```
public class App {
    @Unfinished(message = "Make sure that this element is not null")
    String size;

    @Unfinished
    public static void main(String[] args) {
        System.out.println("Hello World annotation!");
    }
}
```

Although our annotation already looks like a standard annotation, it is not yet operational. For this, a class called processor must be available to the compiler. This class will describe the action to take when an item is annotated with our custom annotation.

To achieve a custom processor for Java 6 annotation, we mainly need to implement the process() method of the javax.annotation.processing.Processor interface and define the annotations supported by this processor with the @SupportedAnnotationTypes annotation. The following code shows the processor of our custom Unfinished annotation. As you can see, for the implementation of the process() method, we used the abstract class AbstractProcessor that implements the Processor interface. (This prevents us from having to implement all the methods defined in this interface.)

```
@SupportedAnnotationTypes("com.packt.ch07.annotations.Unfinished")
public class UnfinishedProcessor extends AbstractProcessor {

  /**
   * For the ServiceLoader
   */
  public UnfinishedProcessor() {
  }

  @Override
  public boolean process(Set<? extends TypeElement>
    annotations, RoundEnvironment roundEnv) {
    try {
      //For each annotated element do ...
      for (Element e :
        roundEnv.getElementsAnnotatedWith(Unfinished.class)) {
        Unfinished unf = e.getAnnotation(Unfinished.class);
        System.out.println("***** Class :
          "+e.getEnclosingElement()+", "
          + "Annotated element : " + e.getSimpleName()+", "
          + " Kind : "+e.getKind()+", Message :
          "+unf.message()+"**** ");
      }
    } catch (Exception ex) {
      ex.printStackTrace();
    }
    return true;
  }
}
```

Once the processor is realized, we must now declare it so that it can be found by the compiler. The simplest way to do this is to use the Java mechanism for services declarations using the following steps:

1. Package your annotation in a JAR file.

2. Include a META-INF/services directory in this JAR file.

3. Include a file named javax.annotation.processing.Processor in the META-INF/services directory.

4. Specify in this file the fully qualified names of the processors contained in the JAR file (one processor per line).

The following screenshot shows the structure of the project that contains the Unfinished annotation. Failing to put the annotation and the processor in the same project as is the case of our example, you can use one project for annotations and another for processors. But whatever your option, do not forget to define the service in the META-INF/services project directory that contains the processor.

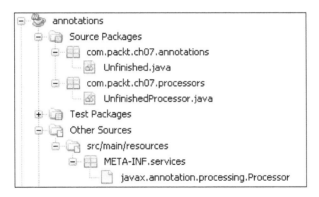

The following screenshot shows the contents of the file javax.annotation. processing.Processor. As the package contains only a single processor, then it is obvious that we will have a single line in this file as shown in the following screenshot:

```
1    com.packt.ch07.processors.UnfinishedProcessor
```

For those using **Maven v2.3.2**, to achieve the project that contains the processors, they must set the option <compilerArgument>-proc:none</compilerArgument> in the configuration of the plugin maven-compiler-plugin so that the code is properly compiled.

Now you can import the package that contains the annotation in another project and use it at your convenience. When compiling our preceding `App` class, we have the following result:

```
***** Class :com.packt.ch07.App, Annotated element : size,  Kind :
FIELD, Message : Make sure that this element is not null****
***** Class :com.packt.ch07.App, Annotated element : main,  Kind :
METHOD, Message : Nothing has been done****
```

Latest improvements in action

Affected by maintenance release, the common annotation specification has not greatly changed. We have in all, the addition of a new annotation and update of some sections of the specification document.

The new annotation

The new annotation that was added to the specification concerns the management of priorities when using a series of classes in a given order. This is the `javax.annotation.priority` annotation.

The exact role and the ranges of acceptable values for this annotation are defined by each specification that uses it.

For example, this annotation could be used to manage the execution order of interceptors.

Contexts and Dependency Injection

The Contexts and Dependency Injection(CDI) for Java EE 1.1 Specification was developed under JSR 346. This section just gives you an overview of improvements in the API. The complete document specification (for more information) can be downloaded from `http://jcp.org/aboutJava/communityprocess/final/jsr346/index.html`.

What is CDI ?

Introduced in the Java EE platform from Version 6, Contexts and Dependency Injection for Java EE (CDI) is a specification that has brought to the platform a set of services that simplify the management of the lifecycle of objects, and standardize and encourage the use of dependency injection in the Java EE environment. In concrete terms, this specification gives us the ability to easily link in a loosely coupled and type-safe way the different layers (presentation, business and data access) of n-tier architectures. In order to do this, the CDI primarily relies on two services that are:

- **Context**: This is used for the management of the lifecycle of the objects (the time of creation and destruction) based on their scope.

- **Dependency Injection**: This includes a number of elements such as the injection of a component into another, the choice of implementation to be injected for a given interface and the type of object provided to access the injected dependence: a proxy or a reference that gives direct access to the instance.

To get a better idea of the power of CDI, let us take some examples.

Example 1 – instantiation of a POJO

Suppose we have a JSF managed bean that wants to access an instance of a POJO that implements an interface. The basic approach is to create an instance of the POJO in the managed bean by using the new keyword as is the case in the following code:

```
@ManagedBean
public class MyManagedBean {

  IHelloWorld hw = new HelloWorld();

  public String getMyHelloWorld(){
    return hw.getHelloWorld();
  }
}
public class HelloWorld implements IHelloWorld{

  @Override
  public String getHelloWorld() {
    return "Hello World";
  }
}
```

The drawback with this approach is that the instance of the HelloWorld class is created in hard code, which causes a very strong coupling between the managed bean and implementation of IHeloWorld interface. Therefore, to change IHelloWorld implementation, you must have an access to the managed bean and modify it.

With the CDI, the managed bean will just declare a dependency on an IHelloWorld instance and inject it. This gives us the following code:

```
@ManagedBean
public class MyManagedBean {

    @Inject
    IHelloWorld hw;

    public String getMyHelloWorld(){
        return hw.getHelloWorld();
    }
}
```

The CDI will look for the implementation of the IHelloWorld interface, instantiate and inject it. Better still, the CDI will take care of managing the lifecycle of the bean that will be injected. Thus, to change the implementation of IHelloWorld interface, we just have to change the class HelloWorld. We will complete our code by specifying the scope of the POJO with @RequestScoped annotation.

```
@RequestScoped
public class HelloWorld implements IHelloWorld{
  //...
}
```

Example 2 – accessing an EJB from a JSF page

Suppose we have a JSF page where we want to access a method of an EJB component. The typical scenario requires you to first access an instance of the EJB from the managed bean associated with the JSF page and then call the EJB method in a managed bean method that will be called in the JSF page. In terms of code that can be translated as shown in the following code.

The following code is an example of an EJB component:

```
@Stateless
public class MyEJB implements IMyEJB{
  public String getHelloWorld(){
    return "Hello world By EJB";
  }
}
```

The following code is an example of a JSF-managed bean:

```
@ManagedBean
public class MyManagedBean {

  @EJB
  IMyEJB ejb;

  public String getMyEjbHelloWorld(){
    return ejb.getHelloWorld();
  }
}
```

From a JSF page, we can call the method `myEjbHelloWorld`.

```
Hello EJB
<br/>
The message : #{myManagedBean.myEjbHelloWorld}
```

With CDI, we do not necessarily need to go through a managed bean to access the methods of an EJB. In fact, we only need to add the `@Named` annotation to our EJB component and it will be accessed from our JSF page like a simple JSF-managed bean. The difference between the two annotations (`@Named` and `@ManagedBean`) is visible in at least two points: the first point concerns the scope. Indeed, the `@ManagedBean` annotation is specific to the JSF Specification while the `@Named` annotation can create managed beans accessible to a greater number of specifications (including JSF) and provides more flexibility in the handling of JavaBean components. The second point relates to the features available to the component. The `@Named` annotation allows you to create CDI beans, which gives you the opportunity to use features that you will not have access to in a JSF bean, such as: interceptors, `Producer`, and `Disposer`. As a general rule, it is advisable to use CDI beans whenever possible.

The following code shows an EJB component annotated with CDI `@Named` annotation:

```
@Named
@Stateless
public class MyEJB implements IMyEJB {
  //...
}
```

The following code shows the access to an EJB from a JSF page:

```
CDI Hello EJB

<br/>
The message : #{myEJB.helloWorld}
```

Example 3 – setting a bean with a specific scope for simple operations

For one reason or another you may want to implement the singleton pattern. In the traditional approach, you will implement a singleton EJB type even if you do not necessarily need all of the services that such a component offers (scalability, roles-based security, concurrency management, transaction management, and others).

With CDI, you can create your bean with the desired scope without the obligation of implementing heavy components for marginal processing. In fact, CDI offers several types of scope that can be defined using annotations (@ApplicationScoped, @RequestScoped, and @SessionScoped). Thus, to implement the singleton pattern without cluttering the services offered by the EJB components, we can simply use the application scope annotation of the CDI as shown in the following code:

```
@ApplicationScoped
public class MySingletonBean {
    //...
}
```

Example 4 – use of objects usually created by a factory

You want to send an asynchronous message via JMS from EJB. The classical approach will require you to instantiate many objects as is the case in the following code:

```
@Stateless
public class SendMessageBean {

  @Resource(name = " java:global/jms/javaee7ConnectionFactory")
  private ConnectionFactory connectionFactory;
  @Resource(name = " java:global/jms/javaee7Queue")
  private Queue queue;

  public void sendMessage(String message) {
    try {
```

```
         Connection connection =
           connectionFactory.createConnection();
         Session session = connection.createSession(false,
           Session.AUTO_ACKNOWLEDGE);
         MessageProducer messageProducer =
           session.createProducer(queue);
         TextMessage textMessage =
           session.createTextMessage(message);
         messageProducer.send(textMessage);
         connection.close();
       } catch (JMSException ex) {
         // handle exception (details omitted)
       }
     }
   }
```

With CDI, all this mass of code is reduced to a line, as shown in the following code:

```
@Stateless
public class SendMessageBean2 {

   @Inject
   JMSContext context;
   @Resource(lookup = "java:global/jms/javaee7Queue")
   Queue queue;

   public void sendMessage(String message) {
     context.createProducer().send(queue, message);
   }
}
```

Latest improvements in action

Having been introduced to the platform from Java EE 6, CDI has become an important solution for component oriented programming in the Java EE platform. Now it only has to spread its tentacles into almost all specifications of the platform so that it can link seamlessly more components and integrate more APIs. In the long list of improvements that have been made, we will present a few including: the possibility of avoiding a bean being processed by the CDI, access to the current CDI container, access to the non contexual instances of a bean, and finally the ability to explicitly destroy bean instances. The improvement of CDI relating to interceptors and decorators will be presented in the next chapter when we will discuss the relevant specification.

Avoiding CDI processing on a bean

Version 1.1 of the CDI Specification came with the annotation @vetoed that prevents an object being considered as a CDI bean. However, a bean decorated with this annotation cannot have a lifecycle similar to the contextual instance. So, it cannot be injected.

By looking at this annotation, some might wonder about its usefulness. To preserve the integrity of some data, it may happen that you need to control the use of some components. But, by using CDI, your components can be manipulated from any other component. Hence the role of the @vetoed annotation. The following code shows us the use of the @vetoed annotation on the Student entity in order to avoid unknown manipulations that can lead to inconsistencies:

```
@Entity
@Vetoed
public class Student implements Serializable {
  @Id
  private String id;
  private String firstname;

  //...
}
```

Accessing the non contexual instance of a bean

This version also added the ability to inject and execute lifecycle callbacks of unmanaged instances of beans. The following code demonstrates how to inject and execute lifecycle callbacks of non contexual instances of the bean Student:

```
Unmanaged<Student> unmanagedBean = new
  Unmanaged<Student>(Student.class);
UnmanagedInstance<Student> beanInstance =
  unmanagedBean.newInstance();
Student foo =
  beanInstance.produce().inject().postConstruct().get();
// Usage of the injected bean
beanInstance.preDestroy().dispose();
```

Accessing the current CDI container

The CDI Specification 1.1 has added the ability to access the current CDI container programmatically and perform some operations. The following code demonstrates how to access a CDI container to explicitly destroy a context object:

```
CDI container = CDI.current();
container.destroy(destroableManagedInstance);
```

Destroying CDI bean instances explicitly

To allow explicit destruction of bean instances in applications, CDI 1.1 has introduced the `AlterableContext` interface, which contains the `void destroy(Contextual<?> contextual)` method. Extensions should implement this interface instead of the `Context` interface.

Summary

After several chapters focused on the realization of a complete system using the Java EE 7 platform, this chapter has allowed us to take a break and try to review some key concepts that we were using. Thus, we learned to make our own annotations and link layers of n-tier applications. In the next chapter, we will continue with the implementation of our application by integrating, this time, the validation of data exchanged between the different layers.

Validators and Interceptors

8

In this chapter, we will see data validation with constraints. This will give us the opportunity to put a small part of **AOP (Aspect Oriented Programming)** in action and discover the novelties in the validation and interception APIs. The specifications concerned are:

- Bean Validation 1.1
- Interceptors 1.2

Bean Validation

The Bean Validation 1.1 Specification was developed under JSR 349. This section just gives you an overview of improvements in the API. The complete document specification (for more information) can be downloaded from `http://jcp.org/aboutJava/communityprocess/final/jsr349/index.html`.

We are almost at the end of the realization of our online preregistration application. In the previous chapters, we developed the different layers of our application and now we need to validate the data that will be handled by this application.

Validating your data

The Java language provides for Java SE and Java EE developers the Bean Validation Specification, which allows us to express constraints on objects. By default, it offers a small number of constraints (compared to the needs that you may have) called built-in constraints (see the following table). But, it gives you the opportunity to combine these constraints in order to make much more complex constraints (custom constraints) that suit your needs. This is what makes its power. This specification can be used in conjunction with many other specifications such as CDI, JSF, JPA, and JAX-RS.

The list of the built-in constraints in Bean Validation 1.1 is shown in the following table:

Constraint	Supported type	Description
@Null	Object	This ensures that the value of the object is null
@NotNull	Object	This ensures that the value of the object is not null
@AssertTrue	boolean, Boolean	This ensures that the value of the object is true
@AssertFalse	boolean, Boolean	This ensures that the value of the object is false
@Min	BigDecimal, BigInteger byte, short, int, long, and the respective wrappers (such as Byte and Short)	This ensures that the value of the object is greater than or equal to the value specified in the annotation
@Max	BigDecimal, BigInteger byte, short, int, long, and the respective wrappers (such as Byte and Short)	This ensures that the value of the object is less than or equal to the value specified in the annotation
@DecimalMin	BigDecimal, BigInteger, CharSequence byte, short, int, long, and the respective wrappers (such as Byte and Short)	This ensures that the value of the object is greater than or equal to the value specified in the annotation
@DecimalMax	BigDecimal, BigInteger, CharSequence byte, short, int, long, and the respective wrappers (such as Byte and Short)	This ensures that the value of the object is less than or equal to the value specified in the annotation
@Size	CharSequence, Collection, Array, and Map	This ensures that the size of the object is in the defined range
@Digits	BigDecimal, BigInteger, CharSequence byte, short, int, long, and the respective wrappers (such asByte and Short)	This ensures that the value of the object is in the defined range
@Past	java.util.Date and java.util.Calendar	This ensures that the date contained in the object is prior to the date of treatment

Constraint	Supported type	Description
@Future	`java.util.Date` and `java.util.Calendar`	This ensures that the date contained in the object is later than the date of treatment
@Pattern	`CharSequence`	This ensures that value of the item meets the regular expression defined in the annotation

One advantage of this specification is the ability to define the different constraints it offers via annotations, which facilitates its use. According to the characteristics of the annotation (explained in detail in *Chapter 7, Annotations and CDI*), you can express constraints for a class, field, or property. The following example shows a `Student` entity whose fields are decorated with the built-in constraints. You can see the constraints to avoid the null value or to define the size and format of attributes in the following code:

```
@Entity
public class Student implements Serializable {
  @Id
  @NotNull
  @Size(min = 1, max = 15)
  private String id;
  @Size(max = 30)
  private String firstname;
  @Pattern(regexp="^\\(?(\\d{3})\\)?[- ]?(\\d{3})[- ]?(\\d{4})
    $", message="Invalid phone/fax format,
    should be as xxx-xxx-xxxx")
  //if the field contains phone or fax number consider using this
    //annotation to enforce field validation
  @Size(max = 10)
  private String phone;
  @Pattern(regexp="[a-z0-9!#$%&'*+/=?^_`{|}~-]+(?:\\.
    [a-z0-9!#$%&'*+/=?^_`{|}~-]+)*@(?:[a-z0-9](?:[a-z0-9-]*
    [a-z0-9])?\\.)+[a-z0-9](?:[a-z0-9-]*[a-z0-9])?",
    message="Invalid email")
  //if the field contains email address consider using this
    //annotation to enforce field validation
  @Size(max = 60)
  @Email
  private String email;

  //...
}
```

Once the constraints are defined, the Bean Validation Specification allows you to validate the data under constraints manually or automatically through other specifications. We begin by presenting manual validation. The following example demonstrates how to validate the constraints of a class manually. We must say that the `Validator` API also provides methods to validate a single attribute or a specific value as shown in the following code:

```
public static void main(String[] args) {
  Student student = new Student();
  student.setEmail("qsdfqsdfqsdfsqdfqsdfqsdf");
  student.setPhone("dfqsdfqsdfqsdfqsdfqsdfqsd");

  ValidatorFactory factory =
    Validation.buildDefaultValidatorFactory();
  Validator validator = factory.getValidator();

  Set<ConstraintViolation<Student>> violations =
    validator.validate(student);
  System.out.println("Number of violations : "+violations.size());
  for(ConstraintViolation<Student> cons : violations){
    System.out.println("Calss :"+cons.getRootBeanClass()+",
      Instance : "+cons.getLeafBean()+", "
    + " attribute : "+cons.getPropertyPath()+",
      message :"+cons.getMessage());
  }
}
```

As we mentioned, the Bean Validation Specification can be combined with other specifications. In the example that follows, we present the coupling between Bean Validation and JSF. We take this opportunity to highlight automatic validation. The example that follows demonstrates how to validate the input of a student in our online preregistration website:

```
@ManagedBean
public class InscriptionBean {
  @Size(min=4, message="The full name must have "
    + " at least four characters!")
  private String name;
  @Past
  private Date birthday;
  @NotNull
  @Size(min=1, max=1,message="Enter only one character")
  private String gender;
  @Pattern(regexp="^\\(?(\\d{3})\\)?[- ]?(\\d{3})[- ]?(\\d{4})$",
  message="Invalid phone format, should be as xxx-xxx-xxxx")
```

```
@Size(max = 10)
private String phone;
@Pattern(regexp="[a-z0-9!#$%&'*+/=?^_`{|}~-]+(?:
  \\.[a-z0-9!#$%&'*+/=?^_`{|}~-]+)"
+ "*@(?:[a-z0-9](?:[a-z0-9-]*[a-z0-9])?\\.)+[a-z0-9]
  (?:[a-z0-9-]*[a-z0-9])?",
message="Invalid email")
private String email;

//...getter and setter
}
```

The following code shows an example of the content of the web page allowing candidates to enter their personal identification. As you can see, we used the pass through attribute explained in *Chapter 3, The Presentation Layer*, to use the calendar of HTML5 and we put the tag `<h:message/>` next to each field with the ID of the concerned field in order to display error messages in case of violation of the constraint. This allows us to have the screen capture shown in the following screenshot.

The following code is an example of the contents of the `identificationInformationPage.xml` JSF page:

```
<html xmlns="http://www.w3.org/1999/xhtml"
  xmlns:h="http://xmlns.jcp.org/jsf/html"
  xmlns:pta="http://xmlns.jcp.org/jsf/passthrough"
  xmlns:f="http://xmlns.jcp.org/jsf/core">
<h:head>
  <title>Inscription information</title>
</h:head>
<h:body>
  <f:view>
    <h:form>
      <table border="0">
        <tbody>
          <tr>
            <th>Name :</th>
            <th><h:inputText value="#{inscriptionBean.name}"
              id="name"/></th>
            <th><h:message for="name" style="color:red"/></th>
          </tr>
          <tr>
            <td>Birthday :</td>
            <td><h:inputText pta:type="date"
              value="#{inscriptionBean.birthday}"  id="birth">
            <f:convertDateTime pattern="yyyy-MM-dd" />
```

```
          </h:inputText></td>
          <th><h:message for="birth" style="color:red"/></th>
        </tr>
        <tr>
          <td>Gender :</td>
          <td><h:inputText value="#{inscriptionBean.gender}"
            id="gender"/></td>
          <th><h:message for="gender" style="color:red"/></th>
        </tr>
        <tr>
          <td>Phone :</td>
          <td><h:inputText value="#{inscriptionBean.phone}"
            id="phone"/></td>
          <th><h:message for="phone" style="color:red"/></th>
        </tr>
        <tr>
          <td>Email :</td>
          <td><h:inputText value="#{inscriptionBean.email}"
            id="email"/></td>
          <th><h:message for="email" style="color:red"/></th>
        </tr>
      </tbody>
    </table>
    <p>
      <h:commandButton value="Submit" />
    </p>
  </h:form>
  </f:view>
  </h:body>
</html>
```

As shown in the following screenshot, when submitting the entry, the contents of the form will automatically be validated and error messages will be returned to the form. Thus, this association (JSF and Bean validation) allows you to define the constraints on a single bean and use it for multiple forms.

The result of the validation is shown in the following screenshot:

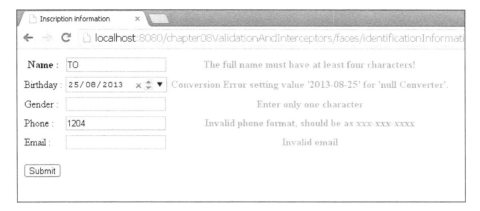

Building a custom constraint

In the previous example, we wanted to have a constraint that allows us to ensure that the value of the `Gender` field was entered in uppercase, but this constraint does not exist explicitly. To do this, we must have some knowledge of regular expressions and use the `@Pattern` annotation. This requires some background. Fortunately, we have the ability to create custom constraints. We will set up a constraint that allows us to perform this task.

The creation of a new constraint substantially follows the same rules as the creation of a simple annotation (as explained *Chapter 7, Annotations and CDI*). The fundamental difference lies in the fact that instead of implementing a processor, we will implement a validator in the case of constraints. That said, the creation of a custom constraint includes the following steps: creating a constraint annotation and implementing a validator.

Creating a constraint annotation

Although the goal is to create a constraint that ensures that a string character is capitalized, we will create a generic annotation. This annotation will take as parameter the type of the expected case. Thus, it may, in the future, allow us to test if the characters are uppercase or lowercase .

We will create the enumeration `CaseType`, which contains different types of case, as shown in the following code:

```
public enum CaseType {
    NONE,
    UPPER,
    LOWER
}
```

Once we have defined the possible types of cases, we will create our annotation and define its characteristics directly. Already, it should be noted that in addition to the basic features we've seen in the creation of annotations, you'll have to add the `@Constraint` annotation that defines the validator of this constraint. For other features, please refer to *Chapter 7, Annotations and CDI*. The following code is the code of our annotation:

```
@Target({ElementType.FIELD, ElementType.METHOD,
    ElementType.PARAMETER,
    ElementType.LOCAL_VARIABLE})
@Retention(RetentionPolicy.RUNTIME)
@Constraint(validatedBy = CaseValidator.class)
public @interface Case {
    String message() default "This value must be uppercase";
    CaseType type() default CaseType.UPPER;
    Class<? extends Payload>[] payload() default {};
    Class<?>[] groups() default {};
}
```

Implementing a validator

Instead of a processor that is required for simple annotations, constraints need to implement the `javax.validation.ConstraintValidator <A extends Annotation, T extends Object>` interface, which provides two methods that are as follows:

- `void initialize(A constraintAnnotation)`: This method is always called before processing a constraint. It allows you to initialize the parameters that will be useful during the execution of the `isValid()` method.

- `boolean isValid(T value, ConstraintValidatorContext context)`: This method contains the validation logic.

The following code shows the validator of our constraint:

```
public class CaseValidator implements ConstraintValidator<Case,
String>{
  private CaseType type;

  public void initialize(Case annotation) {
    type = annotation.type();
  }

  public boolean isValid(String value,
    ConstraintValidatorContext context) {
  if(value == null)
    return true;

    if (type == CaseType.UPPER) {
      return value.equals(value.toUpperCase());
    } else {
      return value.equals(value.toLowerCase());
    }
  }
}
```

After you create your validator, you must register the service (see *Chapter 7, Annotations and CDI*). Then, import the package containing your annotation. The following screenshot shows the structure of the project in which we have defined our annotation:

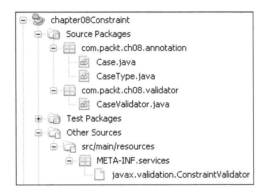

Now, we just need to add @Case (type = CaseType.UPPER) on an attribute of type String to ensure that the value will always be in capital letters. The following code shows the change in the InscriptionBean Bean code that was presented earlier:

```
@Case(type= CaseType.UPPER, message="This value must be uppercase")
private String gender;
```

And the result is simply beautiful, as shown in the following screenshot:

Latest improvements in action

Chapter 2 of the *Bean Validation 1.1 Specification Document* presents the major changes of this version. These are: openness, support for dependency injection, better integration with CDI, support for method and constructor validation, support for group conversion, and finally support for message interpolation using expression language.

Openness

The implementation of the Bean Validation 1.1 Specification has been managed as an open source project. Thus, the source code, reference implementation and test compatibility kit of the API are accessible to the community. For more information, please access the site http://beanvalidation.org.

Support for dependency injection and CDI integration

The Bean Validation 1.1 Specification has standardized the management of objects used to implement validators inside a container and reviewed all the services that were offered to these objects. That helped support dependency injection in Bean Validation components and improve integration with CDI. Henceforth, we can use the @Resource and @Inject annotations to inject objects of type ValidatorFactory and Validator. The following example demonstrates the use of the @Inject annotation to validate an object using Bean Validation components:

```
@Singleton
@Startup
public class InjectValidators {
```

```
  private Logger logger =
Logger.getLogger(InjectValidators.class.getName());

  @Inject
  private Validator validator;

  @PostConstruct
  public void init() {
    Student student = new Student();
    Set<ConstraintViolation<Student>> violations =
      validator.validate(student);
    logger.info("InjectValidators-Number of violations : " +
      violations.size());
  }
}
```

Support for method and constructor validation

The Bean Validation Specification 1.1 has added the ability to define constraints on the parameters of a method or constructor. It also allows the definition of the constraints on the return value of a method. The following code demonstrates how to declare and validate constraints on the parameters of a method and its return value:

```
@Singleton
@Startup
public class ParameterConstraints {
  private Logger logger =
    Logger.getLogger(InjectValidators.class.getName());
  @Inject
  ExecutableValidator validator;

  @PostConstruct
  public void init() {
    try {
      ParameterConstraints pc = new ParameterConstraints();
      Method method = ParameterConstraints.class.getMethod
        ("createStudent", Student.class);
      Object[] params = {null};
      Set<ConstraintViolation<ParameterConstraints>>
        violations = validator.validateParameters
        (pc, method, params);

      logger.info("ParameterConstraints-Number of
        violations : " + violations.size());
    } catch (Exception ex) {
```

```
        Logger.getLogger(ParameterConstraints.class.getName()).log
          (Level.SEVERE, null, ex);
    }
  }

  @Size(max = 2)
  public String createStudent(@NotNull Student std) {
    return "123456";
  }
}
```

Support for group conversion

While cascading a data validation, it may happen that the data to validate belongs to groups that are different from the requested group. For a concrete example, consider the following two classes Student and Address:

```
public class Student {
  @NotNull
  @Size(min = 1, max = 15)
  private String id;
  @Size(max = 30)
  private String firstname;
  @Size(max = 30)
  private String lastname;

  @Valid//To propagate the validation of a student object
  private Address address;

  //getter and setter
}

public class Address {
  @NotNull(groups=AddressCheck.class)
  @Size(max = 10,groups=AddressCheck.class)
  private String phone;

  @NotNull(groups=AddressCheck.class)
  @Email(groups=AddressCheck.class)
  private String email;
  //getter and setter
}
public interface AddressCheck { }
```

To enable the validation of an object step-by-step, the Bean Validation Specification proposes the notion of groups. This gives you the ability to define a subset of constraints that can be validated separately. By default, validation constraints belongs to the `Default` group. And if a validation group is not specified when validating data, only the constraints of the `Default` group will be checked. This justifies the fact that the code of the `testDefaultGroup()` method will run entirely without errors. Although the phone and the e-mail attributes of the `Address` class are not conformed to the constraints, they will not be validated for the simple reason that the constraints that decorate them are not a part of the `Default` group. This can be seen in the following code:

```
public  void testDefaultGroup(){
  ValidatorFactory factory =
    Validation.buildDefaultValidatorFactory();
  Validator validator = factory.getValidator();

  Student student = new Student();
  student.setId("ST23576");
  student.setFirstname("Stelba");
  student.setLastname("estelle");
  student.setAddress(new Address());

  //Only the default group will be test.
  Set<ConstraintViolation<Student>> constraintViolations =
    validator.validate(student);
  assertEquals(0, constraintViolations.size());
}
```

So, to validate the attributes of the `Address` object at the same time as the validation of the `Student` object, you have two options. The first is to list all the groups in the `validate()` method as is the case in the following code:

```
Student student = new Student();
student.setId("ST23576");
student.setFirstname("Stelba");
student.setLastname("estelle");
student.setAddress(new Address());

Set<ConstraintViolation<Student>> constraintViolations =
validator.validate(student, Default.class, AddressCheck.class);
assertEquals(2, constraintViolations.size());
```

The second method is to use the concept of group conversion via the `@ConvertGroup` or `@ConvertGroup.List` for several conversions. As its name implies, this feature gives you the ability to perform conversions from one group to another to validate attributes whose constraints belong to a group different from the requested group. The following code shows the changes that should be added on the `Address` attribute of the `Student` class in order to take advantage of the group conversion feature:

```
@Valid//To propagate the validation of a student object
@ConvertGroup(from=Default.class, to=AddressCheck.class)
private Address address;
```

The following code shows the joint validation attributes of the `Student` object and attributes of the `Address` object after using the `@ConvertGroup` annotation. As you can see in the following code, we did not have to list all the groups of constraints.

```
Student student = new Student();
student.setId("ST23576");
student.setFirstname("Stelba");
student.setLastname("estelle");
student.setAddress(new Address());
Set<ConstraintViolation<Student>> constraintViolations =
  validator.validate(student);
assertEquals(2, constraintViolations.size());
```

The following code shows how to use the `@ConvertGroup.List` annotation:

```
//annotation
@ConvertGroup.List({
  @ConvertGroup(from = Default.class, to = Citizen.class),
  @ConvertGroup(from = Salaried.class, to = Foreign.class)
})
List<Student> studentList;
```

Support message interpolation using expression language

With this version of the specification, it is possible to use expression language when defining the error message. It helps in better formatting of the message and the use of conditions in the description of the message. The following code shows a possible use of expression language in the definition of an error message:

```
public class Department implements Serializable {

  @Size(max = 30, message="A department must have at most {max}
    level${max > 1 ? 's' : ''}")
```

```
    private Integer nbrlevel;

    //...
}
```

Interceptors

The Interceptors 1.2 Specification was developed under JSR 318. This section just gives you an overview of improvements in the API. The complete document specification (for more information) can be downloaded from `http://jcp.org/aboutJava/communityprocess/final/jsr318/index.html`.

Intercepting some processes

Interceptors are a Java mechanism that allows us to implement some concepts of AOP, in the sense that they give us the ability to separate the code from the crosscutting concerns such as logging, auditing, and security. Thus, due to this specification, we can intercept invocations of methods, lifecycle callback events, and timeout events.

Interceptors allow you to intercept method calls as well as the outbreak of some events. During the interception, you can access the method name, method parameters, and a lot of other information. That said, the interceptors can be used to manage cross cutting concerns such as logging, auditing, security (to ensure that a user has the right to execute a method), and modification of the method parameters. You can define them in a dedicated class or within the target class directly.

The signature of an interceptor is as follows: `Object <method_name>(InvocationContext ctx) throws Exception { ... }"` and to `void <method_name>(InvocationContext ctx) { ... }`. It can throw an exception of type `Exception` and should be decorated with an annotation that defines the type of elements it must intercept. For example, `@AroundInvoke` to intercept methods and `@AroundTimeout` to intercept services' timers. Failing to use these annotations, you can always make use of XML configuration.

Defining interceptors in the target class

The following code shows a session bean with method and timer service interceptors. The service timer interceptor (`targetClassTimerInterceptor`) only does the logging, while the method interceptor (`targetClassMethodInterceptor`), in addition to a little logging, demonstrates how to access and modify the parameters of an intercepted method. In this case, we check that the names of candidates start with `Sir`, if this is not the case, it is added.

The following code is an example of a session bean containing interceptors:

```java
@Stateless
public class StudentSessionBean {

  private Logger logger = Logger.getLogger(
    "studentSessionBean.targetClassInterceptor");

  public Student createEntity(Student std){
    logger.info("createEntity-Name of the student :
      "+std.getFirstname());
    return std;
  }

  @AroundInvoke
  public Object targetClassMethodInterceptor
    (InvocationContext ctx) throws Exception{
    logger.info("targetClassMethodInterceptor - method :
      "+ctx.getMethod().getName()+", "
  + "parameters : "+Arrays.toString(ctx.getParameters())+", date
      : "+new Date());
    if(ctx.getMethod().getName().equals("createEntity")){
      Student std = (Student) ctx.getParameters()[0];
      logger.info("targetClassMethodInterceptor -
        Name of student before : "+std.getFirstname());
      if(!std.getFirstname().startsWith("Sir")){
        std.setFirstname("Sir "+std.getFirstname());
      }
    }
    return  ctx.proceed();
  }

  @Schedule(minute="*/2", hour="*")
  public void executeEvery2Second(){
    logger.info("executeEvery2Second - executeEvery5Second - date
      : "+new Date());
  }

  @AroundTimeout
  public Object targetClassTimerInterceptor
    (InvocationContext ctx) throws Exception{
    logger.info("targetClassTimerInterceptor - method :
      "+ctx.getMethod().getName()+", timer : "+ctx.getTimer());
    return  ctx.proceed();
  }
}
```

Defining interceptors in an interceptor class

The following code shows a class that can be used as an interceptor. To complete this class, we extract the interceptor methods contained in the `StudentSessionBean` class. As you can see, this class has no special annotation. But to be explicit, you can decorate it with `javax.interceptor.Interceptor` annotation (in our case, we have not done it to show you that this is optional).

```java
public class MyInterceptor {
  private Logger logger = Logger.getLogger(
    "studentSessionBean.targetClassInterceptor");

  @AroundInvoke
  public Object targetClassMethodInterceptor
    (InvocationContext ctx) throws Exception{
    logger.info("targetClassMethodInterceptor - method :
      "+ctx.getMethod().getName()+", "
  + "parameters : "+Arrays.toString(ctx.getParameters())+", date
    :      "+new Date());
    if(ctx.getMethod().getName().equals("createEntity")){
      Student std = (Student) ctx.getParameters()[0];
      logger.info("targetClassMethodInterceptor - Name of student
        before : "+std.getFirstname());
      if(!std.getFirstname().startsWith("Sir")){
        std.setFirstname("Sir "+std.getFirstname());
      }
    }
    return ctx.proceed();
  }

  @AroundTimeout
  public Object targetClassTimerInterceptor
    (InvocationContext ctx)throws Exception{
    logger.info("targetClassTimerInterceptor - method :
      +ctx.getMethod().getName()+", timer : "+ctx.getTimer());
    return  ctx.proceed();
  }
}
```

The following code shows how to declare an interceptor class in order to intercept some processes of a given class. The result is the same as what you get in the case of the `StudentSessionBean` class presented in the preceding code.

```java
@Interceptors(MyInterceptor.class)
@Stateless
public class StudentSessionBeanWithoutInterceptor {
```

```
    private Logger logger = Logger.getLogger(
            "studentSessionBean.targetClassInterceptor");

    @Schedule(minute="*/2", hour="*")
    public void executeEvery2Second(){
        logger.info("executeEvery2Second - executeEvery5Second - date
 : "+new Date());
    }

    public Student createEntity(Student std){
        logger.info("createEntity-Name of the student : "+std.
getFirstname());
        return std;
    }
}
```

Latest improvements in action

For all the new features added to the Interceptors 1.2 Specification, the most important are certainly: adding of a lifecycle callback interceptor for constructors, adding of standard annotation for managing the execution order of interceptors, and finally, the transfer of interceptor binding from the CDI Specification to Interceptors Specification 1.2.

Intercept constructor invocation

Due to the @AroundConstruct annotation, you can define an interceptor that will run just before the creation of the target instance to intercept the execution of the target instance constructor. Interceptor methods decorated with this annotation should not be defined in the target class.

The following code demonstrates how to use the @AroundConstruct. The example is to record the time at which the different methods have been called to be sure that the method @AroundConstruct is indeed run before the constructor. It also shows you how to access the name of the constructor and its parameters.

```
public class AroundConstructInterceptor {
  private Logger logger = Logger.getLogger(
    "AroundConstructInterceptor.interceptorClass");

  @AroundConstruct
  public Object initialize
    (InvocationContext ctx) throws Exception{
    logger.info("initialize - constructor :
      "+ctx.getConstructor()+", "
```

```
      + "parameters : "+Arrays.toString(ctx.getParameters())+","
      + " execution time : "+new Date());
      return ctx.proceed();
    }
}


@Stateless
@Interceptors(AroundConstructInterceptor.class)
public class AroundConstructBean   {

  private Logger logger = Logger.getLogger(
  "AroundConstructManagedBean.interceptorClass");

  public AroundConstructBean(){
    logger.info("AroundConstructManagedBean - Execution time :
      "+new Date());
  }
}
```

Associating an interceptor with a class using interceptor binding

Associating Interceptors using Interceptor Bindings, Chapter 3 of the *Interceptors 1.2 Specification Document*, was extracted from Chapter 9 of the *CDI Specification Document*. It discusses the possibility of using annotations to associate interceptors with another component that is not an interceptor. To make this possible you must: create an interceptor binding type, declare the interceptor bindings, and bind this interceptor to the desired component.

Creation of interceptor binding types

The interceptor binding type is created exactly like a simple annotation, except that it adds at least the @InterceptorBinding among the annotations used to define the characteristic of the interceptor binding. The following code shows the declaration of an interceptor binding type to log some information:

```
@InterceptorBinding
@Target({ElementType.TYPE, ElementType.METHOD})
@Retention(RetentionPolicy.RUNTIME)
public @interface Log {
}
```

Declaring interceptor binding

We can declare interceptor binding by annotating an interceptor with the interceptor binding type and the `@javax.interceptor.Interceptor` annotation. The following code demonstrates how to declare an interceptor binding:

```
@Log
@Interceptor
public class LoggerInterceptor {
  // Interceptors methods
}
```

Binding an interceptor by using interceptor binding type

After all these operations, it is up to you to decorate a non interceptor component with the interceptor binding types to bind the interceptor to a component. The following code demonstrates how to bind the `LoggerInterceptor` interceptor to our EJB:

```
@Stateless
@Log
public class StudentSessionBeanWithoutInterceptor {
    //Method to intercept
}
```

By default, the interceptor is not enabled. To do this, you must declare the interceptor in the `bean.xml` file as follows:

```
<interceptors>
    <class>com.packt.ch08.bean.LoggerInterceptor</class>
</interceptors>
```

Defining the execution order of interceptors

When we talked about the CDI Specification in the *Chapter 7, Annotations and CDI*, we discussed adding the `@Priority` annotation. This annotation was adopted by the Interceptors 1.2 Specification and permits us to define an execution order for interceptors that were declared with interceptor bindings. When using this annotation, the interceptor with the smallest priority is called first. The following code demonstrates how to use this annotation. In our case, the `LoggerInterceptor` interceptor will be called before the `LoggerInterceptor1` interceptor.

```
@Log
@Interceptor
@Priority(2000)
public class LoggerInterceptor {
    // interceptor method
```

```
}

@Log1
@Interceptor
@Priority(2050)
public class LoggerInterceptor1 {
  //Interceptor method
}

@Stateless
@Log1
@Log
public class StudentSessionBeanWithoutInterceptor {
    //Methods to intercept
}
```

In parallel to this the annotation permits us to enable the interceptors. In other words, it saves you from using the `<interceptors>` element in the `bean.xml` file as we did in the preceding case.

Summary

At the end of this chapter, we are now able to validate inputs on JSF forms and the data that will be manipulated by an application through the Bean Validation Specification. We also learned how to intercept different types of processes such as the creation of an object, invocation of a method, or service timer execution in order to audit or modify a method's parameters. In the next chapter, we will end our journey into the Java EE 7 world by addressing the security aspect of our online preregistration application.

9
Security

We will finish up our project by securing it with Java EE solutions. But first, we will analyze the improvements in the concerned APIs. The development of this chapter will be focused on JASPIC 1.1.

JASPIC 1.1

The **Java Authentication SPI for Containers (JASPIC)** Specification was developed under JSR 196. This section just gives you an overview of improvements in the API. For more information, the complete document specification can be downloaded from `http://jcp.org/aboutJava/communityprocess/final/jsr349/index.html`.

Secure access to forms

Also called JASPI, the JASPIC Specification defines a set of standard interfaces for the development of modules for authentication, which allow secure access to web resources (Servlets, JSP, and so on), among others. Generally speaking, the JASPIC Specification was designed for message-level security; this means that JASPIC modules are called to be integrated into message processing containers and thus, offer a transparent secured mechanism for protocols such as SOAP and HttpServlet.

Implementing an authentication module

In the case where you don't want to use a predefined authentication module, the JASPIC Specification allows you to develop your own modules. This requires the implementation of the `javax.security.auth.message.module.ServerAuthModule` interface. For reasons that we will explain later, you may need to implement the following interfaces:

- `javax.security.auth.message.config.ServerAuthConfig`

- `javax.security.auth.message.config.ServerAuthContext`

- `javax.security.auth.message.config.AuthConfigProvider`

Implementing the ServerAuthModule interface

The `ServerAuthModule` interface contains five methods that must be implemented by the authentication module. These methods are the following:

- `initialize()`: This method is used to initialize the module and retrieve objects necessary for the validation of access to resources.

- `getSupportedMessageTypes()`: This method returns an array of objects designating message types supported by the module. For example, for a module that will be compatible with a Servlet Container profile, the returned array will contain the `HttpServletRequest.class` and `HttpServletResponse.class` objects.

- `validateRequest()`: This method is called by the container whenever an `HttpServletRequest` is received for processing of the incoming message. For this purpose, it receives from the container `HttpServletRequest` and `HttpServletResponse` objects in the `MessageInfo` parameter. At the end of request processing, this method must return a status that determines the sequence of operations in the container.

- `secureResponse()`: This method is called by the container at the time of returning a response to a client. Very often, it should return the status `SEND_SUCCESS`.

- `cleanSubject()`: This method is used to remove one or several principles of a subject argument.

The following code provides an example implementation of the `ServerAuthModule` interface methods:

```
public class ServerAuthModuleImpl implements ServerAuthModule {

    private MessagePolicy requestPolicy;
```

```
    private CallbackHandler handler;
    public void initialize(MessagePolicy requestPolicy, MessagePolicy
responsePolicy, CallbackHandler handler, Map options) throws
AuthException {
        this.requestPolicy = requestPolicy;
        this.handler = handler;
    }


    public Class[] getSupportedMessageTypes() {
        return new Class[]{HttpServletRequest.class,
HttpServletResponse.class};
    }


    public AuthStatus validateRequest(MessageInfo messageInfo, Subject
clientSubject, Subject serviceSubject) throws AuthException {
        try {

            String username = validation(messageInfo, clientSubject);
            if (username == null && requestPolicy.isMandatory()) {

                HttpServletRequest request = (HttpServletRequest)
messageInfo.getRequestMessage();

                HttpServletResponse response = (HttpServletResponse)
messageInfo.getResponseMessage();

                String header = "Basic" + " realm=\"" + request.
getServerName() + "\"";
                response.setHeader("WWW-Authenticate", header);

                response.setStatus(HttpServletResponse.SC_
UNAUTHORIZED);
                return AuthStatus.SEND_CONTINUE;
            }

            handler.handle(new Callback[]{
                new CallerPrincipalCallback(clientSubject,
username)});
            if (username != null) {
                messageInfo.getMap().put("javax.servlet.http.
authType", "ServerAuthModuleImpl");
            }

            return AuthStatus.SUCCESS;
```

```
        } catch (Exception e) {
            e.printStackTrace();
            throw new AuthException(e.getMessage());
        }
    }

    public String validation(MessageInfo mInfo, Subject cSubject)
throws Exception {
        HttpServletRequest request = (HttpServletRequest) mInfo.
getRequestMessage();

        String headerAutho = request.getHeader("authorization");

        if (headerAutho != null && headerAutho.startsWith("Basic")) {

            headerAutho = headerAutho.substring(6).trim();

            String decodedAutho = new String(Base64.
decode(headerAutho.getBytes()));

            int colon = decodedAutho.indexOf(':');
            if (colon <= 0 || colon == decodedAutho.length() - 1) {
                return null;
            }

            String username = decodedAutho.substring(0, colon);
            String password = decodedAutho.substring(colon + 1);

            //Container password validation, you can put your
            //own validation process instead of delegating it to the
container
            PasswordValidationCallback pwdValidCallback =
                    new PasswordValidationCallback(cSubject, username,
password.toCharArray());

            handler.handle(new Callback[]{pwdValidCallback});
            //Removes the stored password
            pwdValidCallback.clearPassword();
```

```
                password = null;

            if (pwdValidCallback.getResult()) {//if the user is
authenticated
                return username;
            }
        }
        return null;
    }

    public AuthStatus secureResponse(MessageInfo messageInfo, Subject
serviceSubject) throws AuthException {
        return AuthStatus.SEND_SUCCESS;
    }

    public void cleanSubject(MessageInfo messageInfo, Subject subject)
throws AuthException {
    }
}
```

Installing and configuring the authentication module

Install the authentication module by copying the JAR file of the module in the `install_glassfish\ glassfish\domains\domain1\lib` directory of your GlassFish Server.

Once the module is installed, you can configure it in the GlassFish administration console as follows:

1. Log on to the GlassFish administration console.
2. Expand the **server-config** menu.
3. In the menu that appears, expand the **Security** menu.
4. In the submenu, expand the **Message security** menu.
5. Click on the **HttpServlet** menu.
6. On the form that appears, click on the **Providers** tab to add a new provider.

7. Click on the **New** button and fill out the appropriate form. Before recording your entry, your form should look like the following screenshot:

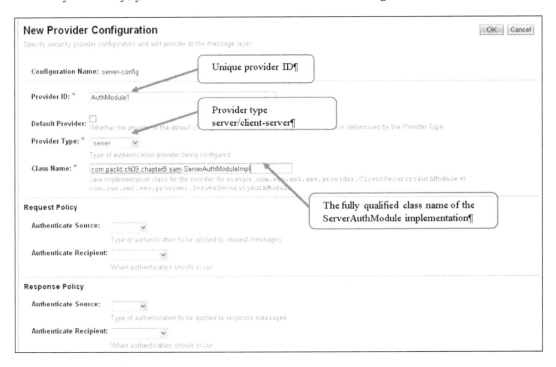

Binding the authentication module to a web application

To bind an authentication module to an application, you have two options in GlassFish:

- The first option (which is by far the simplest) is to configure the `httpservlet-security-provider` attribute of the element `glassfish-web-app` in the `glassfish-web.xml` file of the application. The purpose of this configuration is to make you use the `AuthConfigProvider` implementation provided by GlassFish to instantiate your security module. The following code shows the contents of the `glassfish-web.xml` file of our application. As you can see, we passed the ID of our provider to the `httpservlet-security-provider` attribute. Thus, whenever it is necessary to analyze the security of a request, the GlassFish server through its `AuthConfigProvider` implementation will instantiate our security module in order to make it operational.

```
<glassfish-web-app error-url=""  httpservlet-security-
provider="AuthModule1">
  <class-loader delegate="true"/>
</glassfish-web-app>
```

- The second method is to implement your own implementation of the `AuthConfigProvider` interface. Therefore, in this case, you need to implement `javax.security.auth.message.config.ServerAuthConfig`, `javax.security.auth.message.config.ServerAuthContext`, and `javax.security.auth.message.config.AuthConfigProvider` interfaces. For those who are thrilled about the adventure, you will find all the necessary information in this blog: `http://arjan-tijms.blogspot.com/2012/11/implementing-container-authentication.html`.

Creating a realm

We will tell the GlassFish server where all the associated users and groups that can access the secure sections of our application are stored. In other words, we will configure the realm of our application.

For your information, GlassFish provides the ability to define several types of realms. They are listed as follows:

- The `file` realm, for storing user information in files. This is the default realm.
- The `ldap` realm, for storage in an LDAP directory server.
- The `jdbc` realm, for storing in a database.
- The `solaris` realm, for authentication management based on Solaris username and password.
- The `certificate` realm, for authentication management using certificates.
- And if none of these realms satisfy your need, don't worry; GlassFish offers the possibility of creating your own realm.

In our case, we opt for the `jdbc` realm; we need a database structure to store the necessary information (the user name, its password, and the group to which it belongs). The following screenshot shows the structure of tables in which our information is stored:

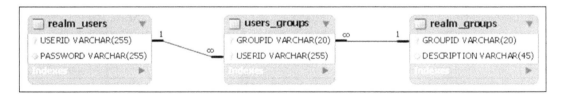

The `realm_users` table will store all user IDs and passwords, the `realm_groups` table will store all the group IDs of our application with their description, while the `users_groups` table will tell us what groups a user belongs to. Thus, a user can belong to several groups.

Once you have defined the structure of the database that will host different users, you must configure GlassFish so that it can connect to your database (MySQL 5, in our case) and access authentication information. To do this, you have to start by copying the Java connector of your database (`mysql-connector-java-5.1.23-bin.jar`, in our case) into the directory: `glassfish_install_dir\glassfish\domains\domain1\lib`. Then, you have to connect to the GlassFish administration console and gain access to the realms creation form by navigating to **Configurations | server-config | Security | Realms**. By clicking on the **Realms** menu, the following form will be displayed; you then need to click on the **New** button and the realms creation form will appear:

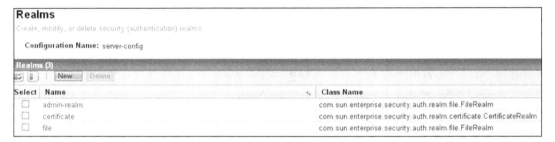

The following table shows the fields that you need to fill for a `JDBCRealm`:

Field	Example value	Description
Name	`MyJDBCRealm`	The name of the realm that will be used to configure security in application
Class Name	`com.sun.enterprise.security.auth.realm.jdbc.JDBCRealm`	The class that implements the realm to configure, in our case, `JDBCRealm`
JAAS Context	`jdbcRealm`	JAAS (Java Authentication and Authorization Service) context ID
JNDI	`jdbcRealmDataSource`	The JNDI name of the JDBC Resources to connect to the database containing the realm
User Table	`realm_users`	The name of the table containing the list of system users with their passwords

Field	Example value	Description
User Name Column	USERID	The name of the column containing the ID of the user in the table `realm_users`
Password Column	PASSWORD	The name of the column containing the passwords of users
Group Table	users_groups	The name of the table that associates groups and users
Group Table User Name Column	USERID	The name of the column in the association table containing the ID of the user
Group Name Column	GROUPID	The name of the column in the association table containing the identifier of the group
Password Encryption Algorithm	SHA-256	To set the password encryption algorithm
Digest Algorithm	SHA-256 (even if it is the default value)	

After filling the form, you can save your realm. With this configuration, we can now use the password validation mechanisms provided by the container to validate incoming connections. This is what we have done in the validation method using the following statement:

```
PasswordValidationCallback pwdValidCallback = new PasswordValidationCa
llback(cSubject, username, password.toCharArray());
```

Apart from using the container validation mechanism, you can access your database and make this validation yourself.

Security configuration

To configure the security of an application, you will need to do the following:

1. Determine the different roles of the application and declare them in web. xml. In our application, we only need an administrator role to perform batch processing and some administrative tasks. The following code demonstrates how to create a role named admin for this purpose:

```
<security-role>
   <role-name>admin</role-name>
</security-role>
```

2. Map URL patterns to appropriate roles in the `web.xml` file. This will define the forms that each role can access. Before performing this configuration, you must group the forms depending on the access constraints you want to define. In the case of our application, we have grouped the forms into two folders: a folder for preregistration forms in the registration folder and another folder for administration forms in the administration folder. Thus, to ensure that only users of the admin role will have access to the administration forms, we will associate the URL pattern `/faces/administration/*` to the `admin` role. The following code demonstrates how to define a constraint that associates the URL pattern `/faces/administration/*` to the `admin` role (the word `faces` of the previous pattern represents the pattern defined in the `<servlet-mapping>` element of the `web.xml` file).

```
<security-constraint>
        <display-name>Constraint1</display-name>
        <web-resource-collection>
            <web-resource-name>Administration</web-resource-name>
            <url-pattern>/faces/administration/*</url-pattern>
        </web-resource-collection>
        <auth-constraint>
            <role-name>admin</role-name>
        </auth-constraint>
</security-constraint>
```

3. Associate each role with a user group in the `glassfish-web.xml` file. In the realm, each user is associated with a user group. However, the URL patterns are associated with roles. So, you need to tell the server which group a role belongs to. In GlassFish, this is possible through the `<security-role-mapping>` element. The following code shows the complete contents of the `glassfish-web.xml` file with the role-group combination:

```
<glassfish-web-app error-url="" httpservlet-security-
provider="AuthModule1">
  <security-role-mapping>
    <role-name>admin</role-name>
    <group-name>administrator</group-name>
  </security-role-mapping>
  <class-loader delegate="true"/>
</glassfish-web-app>
```

4. Declare the realm and authentication types to be used by our application in `web.xml`. The following code demonstrates how to declare the MyJDBCRealm we created in the preceding step. The authentication type we have chosen is `DIGEST`. It transmits the password in an encrypted form.

```
<login-config>
    <auth-method>DIGEST</auth-method>
    <realm-name>MyJDBCRealm</realm-name>
</login-config>
```

Once you complete these configurations, candidates can access the registration forms without any problem. But, if they try to connect to an admin form, a window similar to the following window will be displayed:

Before finishing up this project, you should know that it is possible to customize the login screen and even integrate it into your application. The tutorial at URL: `http://blog.eisele.net/2013/01/jdbc-realm-glassfish312-primefaces342.html` can help you.

The latest improvements in action

The Maintenance Release B of JASPIC Specification has made some significant changes, some of which help to standardize the use of the specification regardless of the server; others help to enrich the user experience. Among the changes, we present only some relatively important changes and advise you to browse the specification document and blog found at: `http://arjan-tijms.blogspot.com/2013_04_01_archive.html`, which will provide you with more information.

Integrating the authenticate, login, and logout methods called

Since Version 3.0 of the Servlet, the authenticate, login, and logout methods have been added to the HttpServletRequest interface for managing the login and logout programmatically. However, the behavior of JASPIC modules after calling one of these three methods was not clearly established. It was left under the care of the server vendors to provide their own method of login and logout. The direct consequence is the non portability of applications between Java EE-compliant servers.

In the recent changes, Version 1.1 of JASPIC has clearly defined the expected behavior of JASPIC modules after calling one of these three methods. We now know that:

- The container implementation of the login method must throw a ServletException when there is an incompatibility between the login method and the configured authentication mechanism.

> Here, the behavior of the module after calling the login method is not clearly defined.

- A call to the authenticate method must call the validateRequest method. This is true if the authenticate method is not called in the context of a call it made to validateRequest.

- A call to the logout method must call the cleanSubject method. This is true if the logout method is not called in the context of a call it made to the cleanSubject method.

Standardizing access to the application context identifier

The application context identifier is an ID used to identify or select AuthConfigProvider and ServerAuthConfig objects for a given application (it is contained in the appContext parameter). Prior to JASPIC 1.1, there was no standard way to get it. As usual, each server vendor proposed a method that was vendor-specific. Now it is possible in standard with the following code:

```
ServletContext context = ...
//...
String appContextID = context.getVirtualServerName() + " " + context.
getContextPath();
```

Support for forward and include mechanisms

The JASPIC 1.1 Specification has insisted on the fact that authentication modules must be able to forward and include during the processing of the `validateRequest` method. Concretely, this is possible by using `request` and `response` within the `MessageInfo` parameter type. The following code gives an overview of a redirection to an error page based on the results of a condition:

```
public AuthStatus validateRequest(MessageInfo messageInfo, Subject
clientSubject, Subject serviceSubject) throws AuthException {

    HttpServletRequest request = (HttpServletRequest) messageInfo.
getRequestMessage();
    HttpServletResponse response = (HttpServletResponse) messageInfo.
getResponseMessage();

    try{
      if(...)
        request.getServletContext().getRequestDispatcher("specificErr
orPage")
                .forward(request, response);
    }catch(Exception ex){}

    return SEND_CONTINUE;
}
```

Summary

Having reached the end of this chapter, which is the last chapter of the book, we are now able to deploy a Java EE public solution with at least some level of security. Indeed, through this chapter, readers become aware of a specification allowing them to restrict access to the forms. However, it is important to note that we have just dealt with one small aspect of security, given the objectives of this book. We ask you to complete your knowledge about security with additional reading. This is because the domain is made up of several aspects such as the transmission of data across the network, method execution, construction, and execution of SQL queries.

Index

Symbols

@AroundConstruct annotation 146
@AssertFalse constraint 130
@AssertTrue constraint 130
@Asynchronous annotation 109
@DecimalMax constraint 130
@DecimalMin constraint 130
@Digits constraint 130
@Documented annotation 117
@ForeignKey annotation 64
@Future constraint 131
@Index annotation 64
@Inherited annotation 117
@MailSessionDefinition annotation 96
@Max constraint 130
@MessageDriven annotation 84
@Min constraint 130
@Named annotation 123
@NamedEntityGraph annotation 65
@NotNull constraint 130
@Null constraint 130
@OnClose annotation 29
@OnError annotation 29
@OnMessage annotation 29
@OnOpen annotation 29
@Past constraint 130
@Pattern constraint 131
@PostConstruct lifecycle callback method 63
@PreDestroy lifecycle callback method 63
@Provider annotation 110
@Resource annotation 14, 116
@Retention annotation 117
@ServerEndpoint annotation 29
@Size constraint 130

@Stateful annotation 80
@SupportedAnnotationTypes annotation 118
@Target annotation 117
@TransactionAttribute annotation 79, 115
@vetoed annotation 126
@WebServlet annotation 35
@ZipResult annotation 112

A

annotations
  @Documented annotation 117
  @Inherited annotation 117
  @Named annotation 123
  @Resource annotation 116
  @Retention annotation 117
  @SupportedAnnotationTypes annotation 118
  @Target annotation 117
  @TransactionAttribute annotation 115
  about 115, 116
  building 116-119
  for Java platform 115
  improvements 120
  javax.annotation.priority annotation 120
  new annotation 120
  Unfinished annotation 117, 119
annotations, JPA 2.1
  @ForeignKey annotation 64
  @Index annotation 64
  about 64
AOP (Aspect Oriented Programming) 129
API
  simplifying 104, 105

application context identifier
   access, standardizing 162
array 23
Assignment operator(=) 46
asynchronousMethod() 82
asynchronous processing 107
AsyncInvoker 107
async() method 107
AuthConfigProvider implementation 156
AuthConfigProvider object 162
authenticate method 162
authentication module
   application security, configuring 159-161
   binding, to web application 156, 157
   configuring 155
   implementing 152
   installing 155
   realm, creating 157-159
   ServerAuthModule interface,
      implementing 152

B

Batch API
   about 18
   batchlet 21
   batch.xml configuration file 22
   chunk 20
   features 18
   Job 19
   JobOperator 22
   JobRepository 19
   Step 19
Batch Applications
   for Java Platform 1.0 17
   for Java Platform 1.0, URL 8
batchlet 18, 21
batch processing
   about 17
   dedicated API 18
batch.xml configuration file 22
bean
   CDI bean instances, destroying 127
   CDI processing, avoiding 126
   non contextual instance, accessing 126
   setting, with specific scope 124

Bean Validation
   about 129
   constraint annotation, creating 135, 136
   custom constraint, building 135
   data, validating 129-135
   improvements 138
   validator, implementing 136, 137
Bean Validation 1.1
   dependency injection and CDI integration,
      support for 138
   group conversion, support for 140-142
   message interpolation, support for 142
   method and constructor validation, support
      for 139
   URL 9
boolean isValid(T value,
      ConstraintValidatorContext context)
      method 136

C

CandidateSessionBean class 89
CDI
   about 120, 121
   bean, setting with specific scope 124
   beans instances, destroying 127
   current CDI container, accessing 127
   EJB, accessing from JSF page 122, 123
   factory created objects, using 124, 125
   for Java EE 1.1, URL 9
   improvements 125
   non contextual bean instance, accessing 126
   POJO instantiation 121, 122
   processing on bean, avoiding 126
CDI injection 63
certificate realm 157
ChatServerEndPoint class 89
chunk 18-20
class diagram 89
cleanSubject method 162
cleanSubject() method 152
client endpoint 31
ClientResponseFilter interface 110
Collection objects support
   assignment operator(=) 46
   Collection objects construction 44
   collection operations 45

semi-colon operator (;) 46
static fields and methods 47
string concatenation operator (+=) 46
Common Annotations for Java Platform 1.2
   URL 9
Common Client Interface (CCI) 99
component diagram 91
concurrency
   about 11
   and Java EE 12
   benefits 12
   risks 12
concurrency utilities
   about 7
   for Java EE 1.0, URL 8
ConnexionServlet class 35
constraint
   annotation, creating 135, 136
   custom constraint, building 135
container
   CDI container, accessing 127
ContainerResponseFilter interface 110
context 121
Contexts and Dependency Injection. *See*
   CDI
createEntityGraph() method 66
criteria API
   about 69
   bulk update/delete, support 69
   new reserved identifiers, support 70
Customer Relationship Management (CRM)
   99

D

dependency injection 121
DLL generation 70, 72
DOM API 26
dynamic entity graphs 66

E

eagerly 65
EJB
   accessing, from JSF page 122, 123
EJB 3.2, improvements
   EJB Lite improvements 81, 82
   other 85, 86

session bean enhancement 79, 80
   TimerService API, modifications 82, 83
EJBContainer class 86
EJBContainer.close() method 86
EJB injection 63
EL (Expression Language) 42
ELProcessor class 43
e-mails
   sending, in Java 94
   sending, via SMTP protocol 94-96
endpointActivation method 101
endpointDeactivation method 101
Enterprise Application Integration (EAI) 99
Enterprise Information Systems (EISs) 99
Enterprise JavaBeans 3.2
   about 77, 78
   URL 9
Enterprise Resource Planning (ERP) 99
entity graphs, JPA 2.1
   about 63-65
   dynamic entity graphs 66
   named entity graphs 65, 66
   static entity graphs 65, 66
entity interceptor 111, 112
ETL (extract-transform-load) 17
Expression Language 3.0
   about 41
   API, for standalone environment 43
   Collection objects support 44
   improvements 42
   Lambda expression 43
   URL 8

F

Faces Flow 54-56
file realm 157
filter 110
find() method 66
Flash 7
forward and include mechanism 163
FUNCTION keyword 68

G

getAllTimers() method 82
getEntityGraph() method 65
getJobOperator() factory 22

getListOfAllStudentsAs2 method 109
getListOfAllStudentsAs method 108
getOn() method 70
getSupportedMessageTypes() method 152
GlassFish Server 4.0
  URL 8

H

HTML5 7, 8
HttpServletRequest class 40
httpservlet-security-provider attribute 156
HttpUpgradeHandler class 40

I

IHelloWorld implementation 122
IHeloWorld interface 122
IMAP (Internet Message Access Protocol)
  94
initialize() method 152
init() method 79
InscriptionCheckpoint 20
InscriptionValidationBean class 89
inscriptionValidation.xhtml facelet 90
interceptor binding
  declaring 148
  types, creating 147
  type, used for binding interceptor 148
  used, for associating interceptor with class
    147
interceptor class
  interceptors, defining 145
interceptors
  about 143
  associating with class, interceptor bindings
    used 147
  binding, declaring 148
  binding, interceptor binding type used 148
  binding types, creating 147
  defining, in interceptor class 145
  defining, in target class 143
  execution order, defining 148
  improvements 146
Interceptors 1.2
  URL 9

J

J2EE. *See* Java EE
JASPIC 151
Java API
  for JSON Processing 25
  for JSON Processing 1.0 23
  for RESTful Web Services 105
  for WebSocket 1.0 27
Java API for JSON Processing 1.0
  URL 8
Java API for WebSocket 1.0
  URL 8
Java Authentication Service Provider
    Interface for Containers 1.1
    (JASPIC 1.1)
  URL 9
Java Authentication SPI for Containers. *See*
  JASPIC
Java Authorization Service Provider
    Contract for Containers 1.5
    (JACC 1.5)
  URL 9
JavaBeans Activation Framework
    (JAF framework) 94
Java EE
  and concurrency 12
  history 5, 6
Java EE 7
  goals 6
  HTML5 support 7, 8
  productivity 7
  specifications 8-10
Java EE Concurrency API 12-16
Java EE Connector Architecture. *See* JCA
Java EE Connector Architecture 1.7
  URL 10
java.lang.annotation package 117
java.lang.AutoCloseable interface 86
JavaMail
  about 93
  access modifiers, modifications 98
  annotations, added 96
  improvements 96
  @MailSessionDefinition annotation 96, 97
  methos, added 98

JavaMail 1.5
  URL 10
Java Message Service. *See* JMS
Java Message Service 2.0
  URL 9
Java Persistence 2.1
  URL 9
Java Persistence API. *See* JPA
Java Persistence API 2.1
  about 59
  Java Persistence API (JPA) 59
  URL 59
Java Persistence Query Language. *See* JPQL
Java platform
  annotations 115
JavaScript Object Notation. *See* JSON
JavaServer Faces 2.2
  about 47
  URL 9
JavaServer Pages 2.3
  URL 9
Java Servlet 3.1 Specification
  URL 8
Java Specification Request (JSR 342) 8
Java Transaction API. *See* JTA
Java Transaction API 1.2
  about 72
  URL 10
java.util.concurrent.ExecutorService
    interface 13
javax.annotation.processing.Processor
    interface 118
javax.jms.MessageListener interface 84
javax.persistence.criteria.CriteriaBuilder
    interface 70
javax.persistence.schema-generation.con-
    nection property 71
javax.persistence.schema-generation.create-
    source property 71
javax.persistence.schema-generation.data-
    base.action property 70
javax.persistence.schema-generation.drop-
    source property 71
javax.security.auth.message.module.
    ServerAuthModule interface 152
javax.transaction.TransactionScoped an-
    notation 74

JAX-RS 2.0
  about 107
  asynchronous processing 107
  client API 107
  URL 9
JCA
  about 99
  endpointActivation method 101
  endpointDeactivation method 101
  improvements 101
  in action 100
JCP (Java Community Process) 6, 81
jdbc realm 157
JMS
  about 101, 102
  API, simplifying 104
  broker 103
  delivery delay 103
  features 102
  improvements 102
  JMSXDeliveryCount message property,
    handling 104
  messages, sending asynchronously 103
  setAsync() method 103
JMS 1.1 7
JMSProducer 104
JMSXDeliveryCount message property
  handling 104
Job 18, 19
JobOperator 22
JobRepository 19
JPA
  about 59
  in action 60, 61
JPA 2.1
  about 62
  annotations 64
  DDL generation 70-72
  entity graphs 65
  entity listener 63
  JPQL 67
  persistence context synchronization 63
  persistence context, synchronization 62
JPQL
  about 67
  FUNCTION keyword 68
  named queries, creating at runtime 68

ON keyword 68
stored procedures, support 67
TREAT keyword 68
JSF (JavaServer Faces)
about 8, 47
Faces Flow 54-56
HTML5-friendly markup 50
identification page 48
improvements 50
Pass-through attributes 50, 51
Pass-through elements 51, 52
Resource Library Contracts 52-54
stateless views 57
JSON
about 23
array 23
need for 24
object 23
value 24
JSON data presentation 24
JSON processing
object model API 26
streaming API 25, 26
JSP Standard Tag Library (JSTL) 42
JSR-338 59
JTA
about 72
in action 73
innovations 74

L

Lambda expression 43
lazily 65
ldap realm 157
List object construction 44
login method 162
logout method 162

M

ManagedExecutorService interface 13-15
ManagedExecutorService resource
    environment 13
ManagedScheduledExecutorService inter-
    face 15
ManagedThreadFactory interface 15

Map object construction 45
MessageConsumer object 104
Message-Driven Bean (MDB) 84
MessageInfo parameter type 163
Message Oriented Middleware (MOM) 101
MessageProducer object 104
MimeMessage class 94
MyGzipWriterJaxRsInterceptor class 113
MyGzipWriterJaxRsInterceptor interceptor
    112
MySessionBean class 115

N

named entity graphs 65, 66
Non blocking I/O API 36
nonPersistentEJBTimerService() method 82

O

object model API 26
objects
about 23
used by factory, creating 124, 125
oldMethod() method 115
ON keyword 68
onMessage method 84
on() method 70
ONPRINS 87
ORMs (Object-relational mapping)
URL 59

P

passivationCapable attribute 80
persistence context, JPA 2.1
synchronization 62, 63
poisonous messages 104
POJO
instantiation 121, 122
POP3 (Post Office Protocol) 94
process() method 118

Q

query hint 65

R

ReaderInterceptor interface 111
Reader-Processor-Writer pattern 18
ReadListener 37
ReadListenerImpl 39
realm
  certificate realm 157
  creating 157-159
  file realm 157
  jdbc realm 157
  ldap realm 157
  solaris realm 157
realm_users table 158
registerCandidate method 89
resource adapter 99
Resource Library Contracts 52-54
RESTful Web Services
  Java API for 105
resume() method 109

S

secureResponse() method 152
security
  configuring 159, 160
Semi-colon operator (;) 46
ServerAuthConfig object 162
ServerAuthModule interface method 152
server endpoint 29
Servlet
  about 33
  login page with 34
  login with 35, 36
Servlet 3.1
  about 33
  improvements 36
  Non blocking I/O API 36-38
  protocol processing, upgrade 39, 40
ServletInputStream class 38
ServletOutputStream class 38
session bean
  singleton session bean 79
  stateful session bean 79
  stateless session bean 79
SessionContext 116
session object 94
setAsync() method 103

Set object construction 44
SGML (Standardised Generalised Markup
      Language) 24
singleton session bean 79
SMTP protocol
  used, for sending e-mail 94-96
SMTP (Simple Mail Transport Protocol) 94
SOAP (Simple Object Access Protocol) 106
solaris realm 157
startValidationBatchJob method 89
stateless session bean 79
stateless view 57
static entity graphs 65
StAX API 25
step 19
stored procedure 67
streaming API 25
stream() method 45
String concatenation operator (+=) 46
SynchronizationType.UNSYNCHRONIZED
      persistence context 62

T

TCP (Transmission Control Protocol) 28
T find(Class<T> type, Object o) method 61
TimerService API
  modifications 82
T merge(T t) method 61
TREAT keyword 68
treat() method 70
try-with-resources statement 86

U

UCD 88
Unfinished annotation 117, 119
Uniform Resource Identifiers (URIs). 106
Use Case Diagram. *See* UCD
users_groups table 158

V

validateRequest method 163
validateRequest() method 152
ValidationJobListener 89
ValidationProcessor class 89
ValidationReader class 89

ValidationWriter class 89
value 24
void detach(Object o) method 61
void initialize(A constraintAnnotation)
    method 136
void persist(Object o) method 61
void remove(Object o) method 61

W

web application
  authentication module, binding to 156
WebConnection class 40
Web Services
  uses 106

Web Services for Java EE 1.4
  URL 9
WebSocket API
  about 28, 29
  Client endpoint 31
  need for 28
  Server endpoint 29, 30
WriteListener 37
WriterInterceptor implemention 112
WriterInterceptor interface 111

X

XML data presentation 24
XML (Extensible Markup Language) 24

Thank you for buying
Java EE 7 First Look

About Packt Publishing

Packt, pronounced 'packed', published its first book "*Mastering phpMyAdmin for Effective MySQL Management*" in April 2004 and subsequently continued to specialize in publishing highly focused books on specific technologies and solutions.

Our books and publications share the experiences of your fellow IT professionals in adapting and customizing today's systems, applications, and frameworks. Our solution based books give you the knowledge and power to customize the software and technologies you're using to get the job done. Packt books are more specific and less general than the IT books you have seen in the past. Our unique business model allows us to bring you more focused information, giving you more of what you need to know, and less of what you don't.

Packt is a modern, yet unique publishing company, which focuses on producing quality, cutting-edge books for communities of developers, administrators, and newbies alike. For more information, please visit our website: www.packtpub.com.

Writing for Packt

We welcome all inquiries from people who are interested in authoring. Book proposals should be sent to author@packtpub.com. If your book idea is still at an early stage and you would like to discuss it first before writing a formal book proposal, contact us; one of our commissioning editors will get in touch with you.

We're not just looking for published authors; if you have strong technical skills but no writing experience, our experienced editors can help you develop a writing career, or simply get some additional reward for your expertise.

PUBLISHING

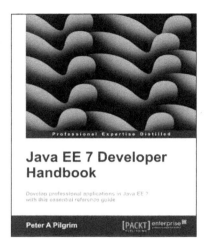

Java EE 7 Developer Handbook

ISBN: 978-1-84968-794-2   Paperback: 634 pages

Develop professional applications in Java EE 7 with this essential reference guide

1. Learn about local and remote service endpoints, containers, architecture, synchronous and asynchronous invocations, and remote communications in a concise reference

2. Understand the architecture of the Java EE platform and then apply the new Java EE 7 enhancements to benefit your own business-critical applications

3. Learn about integration test development on Java EE with Arquillian Framework and the Gradle build system

Java EE 6 with GlassFish 3 Application Server

ISBN: 978-1-84951-036-3   Paperback: 488 pages

A practical guide to install and configure the GlassFish 3 Application Server and develop Java EE 6 applications to be deployed to this server

1. Install and configure the GlassFish 3 Application Server and develop Java EE 6 applications to be deployed to this server

2. Specialize in all major Java EE 6 APIs, including new additions to the specification such as CDI and JAX-RS

3. Use GlassFish v3 application server and gain enterprise reliability and performance with less complexity

Please check **www.PacktPub.com** for information on our titles

Java EE6 Cookbook for securing, tuning, and extending enterprise applications

Packed with comprehensive recipes to secure, tune, and extend your Java EE applications

Mick Knutson

[PACKT] enterprise

Java EE 6 Cookbook for Securing, Tuning, and Extending Enterprise Applications

ISBN: 978-1-84968-316-6   Paperback: 356 pages

Packed with comprehensive recipes to secure, tune, and extend your Java EE applications

1. Secure your Java applications using Java EE built-in features as well as the well-known Spring Security framework

2. Utilize related recipes for testing various Java EE technologies including JPA, EJB, JSF, and Web services

3. Explore various ways to extend a Java EE environment with the use of additional dynamic languages as well as frameworks

Java EE 5 Development using
GlassFish
Application Server

The complete guide to installing and configuring the GlassFish Application Server and developing Java EE 5 applications to be deployed to this server

David R. Heffelfinger

PACKT

Java EE 5 Development using GlassFish Application Server

ISBN: 978-1-84719-260-8   Paperback: 424 pages

The complete guide to installing and configuring the GlassFish Application Server and developing Java EE 5 applications to be deployed to this server

1. Concise guide covering all major aspects of Java EE 5 development

2. Uses the enterprise open-source GlassFish application server

3. Explains GlassFish installation and configuration

4. Covers all major Java EE 5 APIs

Please check **www.PacktPub.com** for information on our titles

www.ingramcontent.com/pod-product-compliance
Lightning Source LLC
LaVergne TN
LVHW062317060326

832902LV00013B/2267